Coerced and forced abortions are more common than most people realize. The same is true of domestic violence. *Healing Hidden Bruises* sheds light on the link between these two terrible problems. But most importantly, this book will take victims through a process of getting safe, free, healthy, and whole.

> David C. Reardon, Ph.D., Founder and Director of the Elliot Institute

"I strongly encourage everyone to read *Healing Hidden Bruises*. Arlene has written and shared truth in an interesting and inspiring way—a way that can change lives. She offers hope, knowledge, and power to those who are suffering."

> Allan Parker, President of The Justice Foundation.*

---

*The Justice Foundation's Center Against Forced Abortion provides free legal resources and training for lawyers, police, school counselors, and pregnancy resource centers and direct legal help to mothers who are being unduly pressured, forced, or coerced into an unwanted abortion. Please contact them immediately if you need help.

"Arlene Lehmann has written a timely book on the pain, cycle, and impact of domestic violence. The church is often viewed as a refuge by victims of abuse. This presents a major opportunity to provide much-needed help, yet faith leaders frequently have little training to truly understand domestic violence. They can unknowingly become a part of the cycle of abuse, and this has exponential generational effects.

Arlene presents the opportunity to recognize the prevalence and importance of domestic violence and to lift the curtain of secrecy. This is an opportunity for the church to be a major part of the help and healing process."

Debbie Stafford, MA, CAS, Full Status Domestic Violence Counselor of 28 Years, and Former Colorado State Representative

Whether one's conviction is pro-life, uncertain, or a strong belief that abortion should be without restriction, everyone should agree that coercion to abort is not only a bad idea, but abhorrent, and that physical abuse in all of its forms is evil. In *Healing Hidden Bruises*, Arlene chronicles her own story of physical and emotional abuse, and narrates the link between her desire not to abort, the pressure, coercion, and controlling behavior she experienced, and later coming to deeply regret her abortion. Through various testimonies, this book unfolds the grief of women who have traveled this painful path and wound up in despair. However, the book is also a testimony of the good news—that there is a sure pathway through God to regaining mental, emotional, and spiritual health.

> Rev. Dr. David Chotka, Director of Spirit-Equip Ministries, Chair of Alliance Pray!, and co-author of *Healing Prayer Is God's Idea*

HEALING HIDDEN BRUISES

How to Recover from the Trauma of Domestic Abuse and Coerced Abortion

ARLENE LEHMANN

Copyright

Healing Hidden Bruises: How to Recover from the Trauma of Domestic Abuse and Coerced Abortion

Copyright © 2022 by Arlene Lehmann

All rights reserved. No portion of this book may be reproduced, stored in a retrieval system, or transmitted in any form or by any means except for brief quotations in critical reviews or articles, without the prior written permission of the publisher.

Scripture quotations marked NIV are taken from the Holy Bible, *NEW INTERNATIONAL VERSION,*® NIV.® Copyright © 1973, 1978, 1984, 2011 by Biblica, Inc.™ Used by permission. All rights reserved worldwide.

Scripture quotations marked NKJV are taken from the New King James Version®. Copyright © 1982 by Thomas Nelson. Used by permission. All rights reserved.

Scripture quotations marked ESV are taken from the ESV® Bible (The Holy Bible, English Standard Version®), copyright © 2001 by Crossway, a publishing ministry of Good News Publishers. Used by permission. All rights reserved.

Scripture quotations marked NLT are taken from the Holy Bible, New Living Translation, copyright © 1996, 2004, 2007 by Tyndale House Foundation. Used by permission of Tyndale House Publishers, Inc., Carol Stream, IL 60188. All rights reserved.

Published by Called Writers Christian Publishing, LLC

Tuscaloosa, Alabama

Print version ISBN: 978-1-7354760-6-3

Important Notice

This book is written primarily for Christian women who have experienced abortion and domestic violence in their lives. I acknowledge that some men are abused by women, but that is not the majority of cases. Relationships can definitely be co-combative. However, this book is written specifically to help women who have suffered domestic abuse, so for that reason, the abuser is referred to as "he" and the victim as "she."

This book deals with issues that can cause hurts to resurface. However, it is for the purpose of dealing with them and being healed of them. I have tried to be respectful and compassionate in addressing these issues. I mean no harm.

I am not a professional counselor, doctor, or psychologist. I am writing from my personal experience of suffering through domestic abuse and abortion trauma, of finding healing, forgiveness, and wholeness, and of working with others who had similar circumstances.

The information given is designed to provide helpful tools that can be used in recovery but is not meant to diagnose or treat psychological or medical conditions. It is not to be taken as psychological, legal, or professional advice.

Frequently, exercises used in this book are for spiritual purposes only. Resources and other information provided are only for general informational purposes, and not intended to be a specific recommendation or solution for the problems or needs of any specific individual.

Some names and details in this book have been changed to provide protection to the victims.

To the many women out there who are trapped by feelings of hopelessness and despair, in abusive marriages or relationships, yearning for a way out. I pray you realize that our loving Father does not want you living in fear, and that He will provide a way out. He is the way maker!

To the many women sitting in church pews, suffering silently, wishing they could take back their "choice" of many years ago, dreading each Mother's Day and every child dedication. I know your hurting heart. So does the Great Physician. He is here to lift your burdens and heal your soul.

May you find your freedom in Him!

Contents

Introduction	15
1. FALLING FOR AN ABUSER	29
The Experience	34
The Abuse Escalates	38
Isolation	41
Recognizing Controlling Behavior	43
Combating the Lies: Lie #1—You Don't Have a Voice	44
Discussion Questions	45
2. BROKEN AND MENDED	47
The Spirit of Control	51
Freedom	54
Women Often Suffer in Isolation	55
My Healing Journey	57
Comforting Others with the Comfort I Received	61
Combating the Lies: Lie #2—You Cannot Tell Anyone Your Secrets	62
Discussion Questions	63
3. JILL'S STORY	65
Beyond High School	67
Moving On . . . From Bad to Worse	68
Desperation	70
Things Begin to Look Up	71
A New Start	75
Do You Need a New Start?	77
Combating the Lies: Lie #3—You Cannot Let Others In	78
Discussion Questions	80

4. **THE DYNAMICS OF DOMESTIC VIOLENCE** — 81
   - Recognizing the Signs — 85
   - Cycle of Abuse — 88
   - Power and Control Wheel — 90
   - Characteristics of Battered Women — 92
   - Abuse and the Church — 97
   - Misuse and Abuse of the Biblical Teaching on Submission — 99
   - When the Abusive Husband "Repents" — 104
   - What is the Right Approach? — 106
   - Combating the Lies: Lie #4 — You Are Trapped in Your Situation — 108
   - Getting and Staying Safe — 109
   - Developing a Safety Plan — 111
   - Discussion Questions — 112

5. **THE TIE THAT BINDS** — 115
   - More on Soul Ties — 120
   - The Root of the Problem — 122
   - The Role of Abuse — 123
   - Other Types of Soul Ties — 124
   - The Nature of Trauma — 125
   - Traumatic Bonding Through Abuse — 130
   - Breaking Soul Ties — 131
   - Combating the Lies: Lie #5—You are Damaged Beyond Repair — 138
   - Discussion Questions — 141

6. **UNDERSTANDING THE GRIEVING PROCESS** — 143
   - The Shock and Denial Phase — 147
   - Anger — 149
   - Bargaining — 152
   - Depression — 161
   - Acceptance — 162
   - Healing Exercise: Getting Honest with the Lord — 163
   - Healing Exercise: Get a Stuffed Animal — 165

Combating the Lies: Lie #6—You Are Stuck in One Stage of the Grief Cycle	166
Discussion Questions	169
7. REBECCA'S STORY	171
Deliverance and Redemption Are Available to All	183
Making the Right Choices Can Start Today	185
God Has Dealt with Cruelty and Pain	186
Combating the Lies: Lie #7—Your Sin Requires You to Be Punished	188
Discussion Questions	189
Conclusion	191
Resources	205
Notes	209
Acknowledgments	211
Publisher's Note: An Invitation to Paradise	215
Recent Releases from Called Writers	219
About the Author	223

Introduction

This book is meant to help women who have been in an abusive relationship, are currently in an abusive relationship, or have suffered from the effects of a coerced, pressured, or forced abortion at the hands of an abuser. The idea for this book began marinating inside of me years ago. I was facilitating support groups in my local area both for battered women and for women who were seeking to heal from traumatic abortion experiences. As I simultaneously led both types of groups, I began noticing that there was a lot of overlap. Many of the women who came to one group also came to the other.

An Undeniable Connection

While it doesn't get mentioned very often in the media, a little research reveals that pressure and coercion to abort is very common, and that there is an undeniable connection between abortion trauma, coerced abortion, and domestic violence.

A study led by Priscilla K. Coleman, Ph.D., and published in the *Journal of American Physicians and Surgeons* (Volume 22 Number 4 Winter 2017) found that 73.8% of post-abortive women who were surveyed indicated that their abortion decision was not completely free of pressure from others. 58.3% reported aborting explicitly "to make others happy." And 28.4% aborted out of fear of losing their partner if they did not abort.[1]

Even pro-abortion outlets are sometimes acknowledging the reality of this widespread issue. For example, in 2017, *The Daily Beast* reported on the issue in an article called "Coerced Abortions: A New Study Shows They're Common." They noted, "For women in violent relationships, somewhere between a third and half report having experienced some form of reproductive coercion. But even for women in relationships that are not violent, 15 percent report experiencing such controlling behaviors, according to a study of 1,300 women published in the journal *Contraception* in April [of 2017]."[2]

It's widely studied and widely reported that murder is a leading cause of death for pregnant women. For example, a recent article by *The Hill* reported that, "Using data from the National Center for Health Statistics from 2018 and 2019, researchers found pregnancy 'was associated with a significantly elevated homicide risk' among Black women and among younger women and girls ages 10 to 24. Two-thirds of homicides occurred in the home – and most involved firearms, according to the study."[3] There are quite a few other studies which highlight this problem. For some reason, violence escalates in abusive relationships when the female partner is pregnant.

A special report called "Forced Abortion in America,"[4] which was published by the website stopforcedabortions.com, compiles information, research, and testimonies from a number of studies, news stories, and other sources. Here are several relevant pieces of information found in that report:

- In 95% of all cases, the male partner played a central role in the decision [to abort].
- 45% of men interviewed at abortion clinics recalled urging abortion, including 37% of married men. They also justified being "the primary decision maker regarding abortion."
- 64% of women who aborted felt pressured by others to do so.

In addition to academic and scholarly studies, there are plenty of legal cases which demonstrate the problem of coerced abortion, and some are highlighted in the report. A few examples are:

- In Florida, Glenda Dowis was charged with forcing her daughter at gunpoint to go to an abortion clinic, where clinic workers called police. According to a staff member, Glenda Dowis said that if Brittany did not have the abortion, "I'm going to blow her brains out." Police said Glenda Dowis told staff to perform the abortion even though her daughter "may seem a bit teary."
- David A. Gillis, 36, was sentenced to 18 months to two years in prison for felony child abuse after he posed as the father of a 16-year-old girl whom he was sexually abusing and signed consent forms for an abortion at an Omaha

abortion clinic. Gillis claimed he was remorseful about the situation, but prosecutors said he continued to write to the girl while in jail and filed frivolous protection orders against her parents.

• Nicholas Griffin, a Florida law school graduate, was sentenced for trying to force his ex-girlfriend to have an abortion. He hired friends to blackmail his girlfriend by threatening to mail copies of a videotape the couple had made of themselves having sex to the woman's family, friends, and employer unless she had the abortion. The woman later gave birth to a girl.

• New York physician Stephen Pack was sentenced to prison after repeatedly stabbing his girlfriend, Joy Schepis, with a syringe filled with an abortion-inducing drug. A witness said that Pack shouted, "I'm giving you an abortion!" as he forced the woman to the ground near a hospital parking garage. Joy later gave birth to a healthy boy.

• In Arkansas, Shawana Pace was within days of giving birth when she was beaten and kicked in the abdomen by three men. She said she pleaded for her child's life as her attackers told her: "Your child is dying tonight." Her baby girl, Heaven, died. Shawana's boyfriend, Eric Bullock, was convicted of planning the attack.

• Andrew Jerome Gaither pleaded guilty to two counts of simple assault for beating up his girlfriend, Belinda Davis, outside an abortion clinic in Washington, DC. Witnesses said that Gaither beat Belinda after she refused to enter the clinic after speaking with pro-lifers outside the clinic. She later gave birth to a healthy baby.

• Jeremy Powell pleaded guilty to forcing his way into his girlfriend's New York house and beating, kicking, and punching her after she refused to have an abortion. The victim, who was three months pregnant, told police Powell said to her, "I'm going to beat that baby out of you."

There are many more examples given in the report. The report also highlights some direct testimonies from victims in order to give them voices. Here are a couple of examples of such testimonies:

"When I told him, he was furious and insisted that the child be aborted as soon as possible... I did not want to kill this baby, but my codependence and addiction to this man won out. I finally made an appointment with the abortion clinic." —Cynthia Greenwood

"He destroyed our apartment ... and told me to get rid of it. Now! The whole time he cornered me ... throwing things and killing me with his words. The abortion ripped me apart. Any strength I had to leave the abuse was torn away from me." —Mary

Countless cases exist of women who have been pressured, coerced, or forced into an unwanted abortion by an abusive partner or family member. The victim in one such case is very well-known, although the coerced abortion aspect of her story is not so well-known.

A Prominent Example

Most people born before the mid-80s remember the name "Lorena Bobbitt." She became a household name in June of 1993 when she cut off her husband's penis and a few minutes later threw it into a field.

Lorena (now Lorena Gallo) was arrested and charged with malicious wounding, and her husband, John Bobbitt,

Introduction

was later arrested and charged with marital sexual assault. According to Lorena, John had raped her and then fallen asleep shortly before the incident occurred. On top of that, Gallo testified to years of psychological, sexual, emotional, and physical abuse by John.

That is the general story known to the public. If you ask most people who were alive at that time, they can give you a similar summation of the details of the Bobbitt saga. However, what most people don't know—because the media basically ignored this part of her story—is that coerced abortion was also a very big piece of the puzzle.

Lorena had grown up in Venezuela before immigrating to the U.S. in 1987. As part of a large Latino Catholic family, pregnancies were one of the most cherished and celebrated of all life events. So when Lorena told John that she was pregnant, she was expecting happiness, celebration, maybe even a party. Instead, she was met with anger and cursing.

Then he demanded that she have an abortion.

Lorena wanted the child, and responded that she would have the child whether he liked it or not. He continued to pressure her and even threatened to leave her if she did not have an abortion. She finally caved into the pressure and had an abortion in June of 1990.

Dr. David Reardon is widely recognized as a leading expert on the abortion experiences of women and their emotional aftereffects. As the defense team was preparing for Lorena's trial, Dr. Reardon learned that John Bobbitt had pressured Lorena into an abortion. The attack had occurred only eight days removed (June 23, 1993) from the third anniversary of the unwanted abortion (June 15, 1990).

Women often experience severe emotional distress

Introduction

around the anniversary of their abortion, so Dr. Reardon wanted to investigate whether there was a link. He contacted the defense team and worked with them on several issues related to the link between the abortion experience and the attack. Ultimately, the defense team decided not to explore this connection in court. According to an article by Dr. Reardon (*The Post-Abortion Review* Spring & Summer 1996) titled "Why the Truth Was Buried," the defense team had several reasons including the fact that they did not want to provoke a backlash from any pro-abortion jurors, and also the fact that they wanted to focus on showing "that John was a brutal wife beater."

So while the unwanted abortion certainly played a major role in Lorena's emotional distress, it was largely ignored by the courts and the media. However, there is an undeniable connection. Dr. Reardon wrote a series of articles after his investigation of the case, which was largely based on Lorena's and John's own testimonies. The series of articles is designed to "show that the key to understanding the many otherwise outlandish aspects of this case can only be found in understanding how Lorena was traumatized by a *coerced abortion*." Those articles can be accessed at the following URL:

http://www.afterabortion.org/the-john-and-lorena-bobbitt-mystery-unraveled/

Some of the most relevant details are in the excerpts that follow (reprinted with permission from Dr. Reardon and the Elliot Institute).

Excerpts from Dr. Reardon's series of articles about the Bobbitt case:

Introduction

At the time of her abortion, Lorena exhibited at least eight of the high risk factors which reliably predict post-abortion psychological maladjustments. The resulting psychological trauma devastated Lorena and created a cycle of violence and abuse, between her and John, which destroyed their marriage. This culminated in Lorena's attack on John's sexuality exactly three years after the abortion--at a time when Lorena was suffering from a major post-abortion anniversary reaction which included anxiety attacks, depression, flashbacks, and psychosomatic symptoms...

On June 15th, 1990, when she would otherwise have been busy planning to celebrate their first wedding anniversary, Lorena had an abortion. To ensure that the deed was done, John accompanied her to the clinic. When she asked him what it would be like, he told her they would stick needles into her arms. Because she was so terrified and distraught, a nurse had to move her away from John, whom Lorena testified was taunting and laughing at her. Despite this and other obvious warning signs, the clinic counselors and the abortionist did nothing to help Lorena, although it was clear that she did not freely want to have the abortion...

The loss of her child was a tremendous blow against Lorena's self-esteem, her idealism, and her dream of having a family "just like my family" in Venezuela. Aborting against her conscience, she was morally devastated. "I couldn't eat," she testified. "I feel like nothing--like the life is over. I feel--I feel like I was falling apart." She lost interest in activities she had previously enjoyed and experienced her first reported case of major depression.

John acted oblivious to Lorena's feelings. According to his perspective, Lorena only felt bad "the rest of the day, and then the next day. By the time we went to bed, she was all right... I hugged her and told her, you know, just to forget about it. It's over you know." He figured that was all there was to it. What more could be said? And so the abortion became something they never talked about again. But this buried pain would continue to manifest itself in other ways.

One of the first ways in which the abortion affected the marriage was in their sex life. Lorena became sexually frigid, a common post-abortion problem. "I didn't want to sleep with him. I didn't want to see him."

Apparently John did not recognize that this sexual withdrawal was a sign of a broken and bruised spirit which needed healing. Instead, he saw her refusals as willful spite. According to Lorena's testimony it was at this time that the episodes of forced sex began. This included at least one case of anal intercourse, which was painful and humiliating for Lorena. Thereafter, she testified, he would use the threat of anal intercourse to intimidate her. (It is noteworthy that John may have been using this non-reproductive sex act as a tool to warn Lorena away from becoming pregnant again without his consent.)...

After the abortion, their fighting became more frequent, violent, and petty...

On June 18th, their fourth wedding anniversary, and three days after the third anniversary of the abortion, Lorena went to visit Dr. Susan Inman, her family physician. She was hyperventilating and complained that she was filled with anxiety and experiencing cramping. She was having gastrointestinal problems. Her hands were shaking, and she couldn't concentrate on her work. She was suffering from insomnia. (All of these are classic symptoms of an anniversary reaction associated with post-abortion PTSD.)...

Lorena's testimony is that when John first awoke he pulled off her underwear and forced himself upon her. She asked, "What are you doing?" and told him "I don't want to have sex." He ignored her and proceeded to rape her. After he was done, he rolled over and went to sleep. She got out of bed, put her underwear on, and went to the kitchen to settle down and get a glass of water. By the light of the refrigerator she saw the knife and began to have a flashback experience in which she remembered the abortion, the fear of "syringes to go through my bones and I was going to die," the first time he raped her, the anal sex, and the "insults and bad words that he told me."

The next thing Lorena is able to recall, in her testimony, is driving.

Finding Healing

Lorena's case provides a very dramatic example of the kind of intense pain and devastating trauma that can occur in a woman who has suffered from both domestic violence and a coerced abortion.

Not all abortion experiences are linked to domestic violence, of course. But as indicated by the data from studies on the topic, it is fairly common for women in domestic abuse situations to feel pressured, coerced, or forced into abortion. In my own work, I began to notice common behaviors and emotions associated with women who had experienced both of these types of events.

Women who go through these experiences often struggle with tremendous feelings of guilt, shame, grief, anger, depression, and trauma. After much prayer and research—and many years of working directly with abused and post-abortive women—I decided to write this book to help women heal from their experiences.

In the following pages, you will find stories of women who endured domestic violence and underwent abortions—often under pressure, coercion, or force. You will read about the pain they endured, but you will also read about how they found freedom, healing, and peace. There are many tools and exercises throughout the book that will allow the reader to find their own freedom, healing, and peace.

Women can read this book by themselves, or they can go through it together with a support group. Parents, friends, pastors, neighbors, and other caregivers might also find it useful as a resource for helping such women.

Don't Let Anyone Steal Your Healing

The enemy sometimes employs trickery and deception to try to keep a person in bondage. One time a lady told me, "I don't know if I want to go through healing because then I will need to speak publicly about what I went through." She had somehow gotten the idea that if she personally healed from her abortion experience, that God was going to require her to speak about everything publicly.

What a strange notion. But I've heard it more than once.

Of course, it isn't true at all. And it's a good example of

Introduction

the kind of lies that will come at us when we're about to get set free. Don't let anything keep you in bondage. Right now, right here, make a determination that you are going to go through the entire process of freedom and healing, and that you will not let anyone or anything stop you.

Combating The Lies of Abuse

In our journeys through life, most of us have made choices and had experiences that led us into a dark pit. We felt like there was no way out. Maybe we felt like we had gone too far and reached the point of no return. Like disaster was imminent. None of those things were true, of course. Instead, what was happening is that we were drowning in thoughts and feelings of hopelessness and despair.

The truth is that there is always a way out. In order to find truth, it's best to look to God's Word.

> Therefore, with minds that are alert and fully sober, set your hope on the grace to be brought to you when Jesus Christ is revealed at his coming.
>
> 1 Peter 1:13 NIV

Our emotions typically stem from our thoughts, which is why the Lord emphasizes the importance of our thought life. There are voices that whisper lies to us, and if we aren't vigilant, those voices can influence our lives tremendously. So, when faced with a lie or a wrong thought, we can either take it captive and replace it with God's truth, or we can dwell on the wrong thought and allow it to influence us.

That means the first thing we have to do is replace those wrong thoughts.

The Apostle Paul was falsely accused, imprisoned, beaten, whipped, stoned, shipwrecked, and snake-bitten. Yet look at what he tells Timothy:

> The Lord will rescue me from every evil attack and will bring me safely to his heavenly kingdom. To him be glory for ever and ever. Amen.
>
> 2 Timothy 4:18 NIV

We can take this statement from Scripture and declare it as a promise of God over our own lives. Jesus will always make a way out of every evil attack against us. In fact, Jesus is the Way, the Truth, and the Life! So where we are trapped, He's the way out. Where there are lies, He replaces them with truth. Where there is destruction and death, He comes in with life and peace.

At the end of each chapter, in a section called "Combating the Lies," we will examine some of the lies and traps of the enemy, take them captive, and replace them with God's truth. Most chapters also have exercises, prayers, and discussion questions at the end. All of these can help facilitate your healing.

May you be encouraged to know that there is hope for a better life, one that is free from the shackles of abuse. And there is hope from the feelings of guilt, shame, secrecy, anger, hatred, and low self-esteem. You can experience that wonderful freedom and hope. God is on your side.

Introduction

My Prayer for You

I pray you will be encouraged to seek healing from the hidden bruises of abuse and abortion trauma. I pray you will find relief from the suffering dealt out to you by fists of anger rather than the hands of love. I pray you will be healed from the harmful, hurtful, and hateful words spoken over you rather than the words of worth, value, and edification. I pray you find healing from the curses that have been pronounced over you. I pray you will find the path of righteousness, which leads you beside the still waters. I pray you will be changed by the power of God that works in you to see yourself as He sees you: a precious daughter.

I pray that as you are changed, your life and circumstances will change, for his word does not return void. I pray you will have the strength and courage to keep fighting for yourself, because you are worth it. I pray that you stand up and claim your right to motherhood, not only for yourself but for your unborn child, who depends on you for protection and nurturing, both inside and outside of the womb. I pray you find your voice and proclaim that you are a child of God and that no weapon formed against you shall prosper. I pray for emotional, mental, physical, and spiritual wholeness. I pray for your soul to be healed from the trauma you have endured. I pray for your abortion-wounded heart to be repaired and restored. I pray you will be empowered to regain control of your life as you surrender to the One Who loves you and gave Himself for you. In Jesus' mighty name, amen.

ONE

Falling for an Abuser

"GET RID OF IT."

Those words still ring in my ears. At the time, his command somehow seemed right to me. It made sense. But there was another part of me that felt like this would not be the right decision.

At that time, abortion was still somewhat shrouded in mystery. There was no such thing as an ultrasound. Young women were sold the idea that their bodies contained nothing more than a few clumps of cells, and proponents of the practice usually referred to the child the same way my boyfriend had: "It."

Still, something inside told me that there was more going on than just the removal of some cells from my body. Unfortunately, by that point in our relationship I had already lost my voice. My boyfriend was in control—he made every decision for the two of us. Of course, our love affair did not start out that way.

It was 1978, and I had decided to break free of small-town life by moving to the burgeoning metropolis that was Denver, Colorado. Like many young people at that time, I had become somewhat fascinated with the Mile High City. The popularity of moving westward seemed to surge after the release of John Denver's song "Rocky Mountain High" in 1973. There seemed to be a gold-rush type of frenzy as people poured into Denver from all over the country.

Moving so far away from home felt daunting, but I did not want to be left out. Denver held promise for the adventure of a lifetime, and at first, it seemed to be fulfilling that promise for me.

Upon my arrival, I took in the sights and sounds of the Rocky Mountains and the city life. Shortly after getting settled into my new apartment, I landed a job for a radio station network that owned both a popular country western channel on the AM band, as well as a popular FM rock station. The job allowed me to meet some people of celebrity status, and others that were up and coming. Some of the artists I met were Buck Owens, Cornelius Brothers and Sister Rose, Huey Lewis and the News, Cheech Marin, and Dennis Weaver, an actor who was starring on the popular television show *McCloud* at that time.

But I was happiest to meet Louis.

Louis was a handsome and charming man, well-educated and successful. He was the news director for the radio station network where I had gotten hired. Several months after I came onboard, Louis asked me out on a date. That romantic dinner turned out to be the beginning of an eight-year relationship.

Soon after we began dating, Louis told me that he was

already dating another lady and had been for quite a while. They were not "officially" broken up, but he had not seen her for six months because she was temporarily living in another state with her sister. She was there primarily to help her sister make wedding arrangements. To this day, I don't understand her decision to do that. I suppose she felt secure enough in their relationship to disappear for six months.

As Louis and I spent more time together and our relationship grew, Louis decided to break up with her. Since she was many miles away, he had to do this over the phone. All of a sudden, her priorities shifted and she was on the next plane to Denver.

After a couple of months of trying to convince him to continue their relationship, she realized it wasn't working. He had moved on. Unable to let go without being the "winner" in the situation, she took another step to try to gain control. Colorado had very liberal laws concerning common law marriage so she decided to sue him.

Of course, all that did was drive him even further from ever wanting anything to do with her again. He was also determined that she was not going to get any of his money. She had come from a very wealthy family and did not need his money at all. It was strictly a power play on her part.

My relationship with Louis continued to grow, but not without growing pains. The lawsuit dragged on for around three years as it made its way through the court system. This was difficult for me because even though I knew he was committed to me, she remained in the picture by living in his house with one of her girlfriends. He hated having her there, but felt that his hands were tied. Louis also hoped that by not fighting her about being there, her anger might subside and she would drop the lawsuit.

Louis once told me that they had gotten into an argument and he had punched her in the chest. She had fallen backward and bounced down the step into the sunken living room. He kind of snickered about it when he told me. This woman was making my life miserable at that time. There was certainly no love lost between me and this woman, but I recall thinking about how bad that must have hurt. I did not see anything funny about it.

There were other incidents that occurred that I wanted to know more about, but he chose not to give me details. He once told me he was trying to shield me from knowing certain things about the lawsuit because he didn't want me to be affected by it. In reality, I think I would have coped with the situation better by knowing what was going on behind the scenes. Even though I did not agree with his decision to withhold information from me, I did not tell him that. Speaking up for myself was not something I was very good at. It seemed like my life was put on hold as we waited for the lawsuit to be over.

Even though I was not living according to my Christian beliefs at that time, they were still important to me. That always gave my internal compass a sense that Louis was really not a good match for me. He made no profession of Christianity. At times, he would also use bad language and vulgarity that I found offensive. To be honest, I hated it with a passion.

Still, I had no family there, very few friends, and basically no support system around me. The result was that we fell into an unhealthy codependent state—something I did not realize or understand at the time. Louis had subtly begun to control me, frequently explaining that he knew what was best for us and I should just do as he said.

A couple of years after I moved to Colorado, my parents came to visit and I proudly introduced them to Louis. This was my moment to show them that I was doing well—that they did not need to worry about me being out here by myself so far away from home.

A few months after their visit, I found out I was pregnant. I was in shock. We had been so careful. Part of me was happy and excited, but another part of me was very frightened. The timing was completely wrong for a baby, especially in the midst of the ongoing lawsuit. Louis's former girlfriend was still vicious and very angry about me, even after almost three years had passed. Neither of us knew what she might try to do if she found out I was pregnant. Since she was still living at his house, that meant Louis wouldn't be able to be there for me the way he wanted to, at least according to him.

It's true that there were ongoing issues. Sometimes when he left home, she would follow him. She would even follow him sometimes even if he was going to do a news story for his job. This was her attempt to make sure he wasn't seeing me. Even though Louis and I were dating openly, she would do anything she could to try to sabotage our relationship or ruin our time together.

Louis was fighting for everything he owned at the time. He told me that if he married me, she would get every penny and then he would not be able to support us. Waiting out the lawsuit seemed like our only viable option.

Since Louis had met my parents and knew of my conservative background, he was aware that it would be shameful for me to be pregnant and unmarried. He also didn't want to put me through the societal embarrassment and challenges that come with being a single mother. Such were the reasons he gave when he announced that we should "get rid of it."

It is hard to think rationally when one is in a pregnancy crisis situation. Many different questions and scenarios run through your mind. I think that is what made Louis's reasoning sound right to me. At the same time, I had this conviction inside that the decision would be wrong.

In the end, what tipped the scales in favor of abortion was the fact that I had lost my voice. Having been told many times by Louis that he knew what was best for me, I had started to operate as though it were true. It had been programmed into me, and I did not argue with him. In some ways, I believe Louis thought he was doing me a favor. My mind mentally consented to his logic, even though my heart knew it wasn't true. With the benefit of hindsight, I can see clearly that my parents would have much rather had their grandchild with me out of wedlock than for me to have an abortion.

My hope is that by sharing my story, I will be able to help other women make the right decision.

The Experience

I walked into the clinic alone.

Louis had been aggressive and proactive up to that point. He had scheduled the appointment at the clinic and had given me the money to pay for it. But now he would sit in the car.

My feeling was very uneasy. I wondered what the procedure would be like. Another young lady sat in the waiting room, nervously turning pages in a magazine so fast that it was clear she couldn't have actually been reading a single word of it. Instead, she seemed to be struggling to occupy her mind with anything that would help her avoid thinking about what was ahead. I sat there quietly, lost in my own scattered thoughts.

This scruffy, kind of sleazy-looking doctor came in, introduced himself, and said he was ready to get started. We often hear the argument that abortion is supposed to be a decision between a woman and her doctor. However, in my case, there was no discussion whatsoever. He came in the room and went right to work.

"We're almost done," I heard the doctor say. "You're doing good." He somehow sounded further away than just being down at the end of the cold steel table. A few moments later, the droning of the machine stopped.

A clinic worker took my hand. Trying to shake myself alert from my groggy state, I asked, "Where's Louis? I need to talk to him."

"He was called back to work," she replied. "He said to call when it was over."

That diplomat must have arrived from England, I thought to myself. *And he has to interview her.* Not wanting to let him off the hook that easily, I reminded myself: *Again, he manages not to be here for me when I need him so desperately.* At that moment, the worker vanished from the room and I was left alone with my thoughts.

Trying to focus again on waking up completely and shaking off the effects of the sedatives, I suddenly had a feeling that something indescribably horrible had happened to me. Something despicable and evil. An emptiness and an intense feeling of fear swept over me. *What am I doing here? How did my life get so out of control?* In better times, I never would have guessed in a million years that I would have ended up here.

The nurse came back. "Could I see it?" I asked. "I want to see it," I quickly added with determination in my voice. For some reason, I all of a sudden needed to see for myself this "blob of tissue" they had removed from my body.

"We don't usually . . ." she hesitated.

"I'd like to," I responded firmly.

Somewhere in the recesses of my mind, I remembered that flier I had seen in college several years earlier. It had pictures of aborted fetuses. At that time, I just thought it was some type of propaganda. But now I wondered, was it really a baby? I had to know. I had to see the remains.

She replied, "Okay. But I can tell you that there won't be much to see. Mostly liquid, perhaps some mass, a little blood . . ."

"Alright."

A couple of minutes later she returned with a small pan in her hands. Struggling to sit up on the pillow, I peered over the edge of the table. My entire body was shaking from the procedure.

My mind eased as I looked at the contents of the pan. It was just like she had described—mostly liquid, a small bit of mass, and some blood. I thanked her politely. My head was reeling and I wasn't at full capacity mentally, but I felt a little better. *No tiny fingers or toes,* I thought to myself. *And nothing that resembles a head as far as I can tell. Maybe it wasn't such a big deal after all. Probably just a blob, like they said.*

But right after I had that thought, the foreboding sense of evil all around me was unmistakable. It was a horrible feeling. Deep inside, there was a void that I wasn't sure would or could ever be filled, and I had the sinking feeling that my life would never be the same.

Right there on that table, I made a vow to God. I told Him that I knew I wasn't living as I should, but that I still considered myself to be His child. And I committed to Him that if I were to *ever* conceive again under any circumstances, I would carry the baby no matter what.

After the abortion, my denial system kicked in. Whatever shred of self-identity or self-esteem that remained before the abortion had been washed down the drain with the life of my child. My life had become a slow but steady downward spiral that included withdrawal, general unhappiness, repression, and then depression. Just a few years prior, I had been a competent and strong-willed young woman who left her roots to travel miles away from home—to what was essentially an unknown land where I knew no one.

Now I was completely and hopelessly dependent on another person—a person who was not healthy or good for me at all. My relationship with Louis deteriorated in the years following the abortion. Although I still cared for him, the relationship was now tainted for me. At the same time, I was too weak to leave him. Fragmented and broken inside, I began to feel trapped.

A couple of years or so after the abortion, I suddenly spoke up during dinner one night. "I sometimes wish I would not have had the abortion."

Louis slammed his fist on the table.

"I wanted that baby!" he shouted.

His outburst took me by surprise. His anger was unexpected and the shouting really startled me. Not knowing how to respond, I just dropped the subject and never mentioned it again. My voice was lost, but my thoughts were in a tailspin. *What!?! He wanted the baby?*

Even now, all these years later, there's no way to make sense of his response. I cannot reconcile his words from that dinner with "get rid of it."

On another occasion, we were at my apartment and got into an argument. Louis again slammed his fist down, this time into my coffee table. He put a hole right through the middle of it. I knew I didn't deserve to be on the receiving end of that kind of anger.

But more important to me at that time, I was upset that he had destroyed the coffee table. It had a special place in my heart because my dad helped me refinish it along with two matching lamp tables that I owned. I explained to Louis that the coffee table was special to me. His only response was to point out that he never liked it. It was clear that my feelings did not matter to him.

I was heartbroken.

The Abuse Escalates

In spite of my lifestyle, I frequently attended church on Sunday mornings during my years of dating Louis. Early on, he never seemed to have a problem with me going. Sometimes I would ask him to come along and he would agree. One time after the service, an argument broke out between the two of us. The minister had said something that Louis didn't like.

After a while, Louis seemed to have something brewing in him. He felt threatened by me spending time with God. He never actually said this to me but I could tell, so I just tried to do my Bible reading when Louis was in the shower.

Louis was a big football fan and would almost always watch Monday Night Football. During one particular game, we began arguing. I don't remember why it started, but the argument escalated to something about cleaning the house. Seemingly out of nowhere, Louis blurted out, "All you ever want to do is read your Bible!" Right when he said that, he swung and hit me in the face with his fist.

He had never hit me before. The physical pain of his fist hurt, but not nearly as much as the crushing blow I felt in my soul. I was absolutely shocked. Not knowing exactly how to react, I remember wanting to tell him that he better not ever hit me again.

However, I was too weak. I remained silent, not realizing that I had completely lost control of my life to this man.

Time dragged on for me, as did our relationship. My life had been put on hold all this time, so I began trying to figure out how I could end the relationship. One weekend, I saw my opportunity. We had a big argument and I decided that enough was enough. I was leaving.

Grabbing my belongings from his house, I took them and threw them into my car. He followed me and began slapping me, yelling, and then punching me with his fist.

"Where do you think you are going?" he roared.

I felt trapped.

Reluctantly, I finally gave in to his demands and unloaded the car.

Several months later, we had yet another argument. I can't recall what started it, but I remember that the argument lasted for hours. It began in the morning on a Saturday and went late into the afternoon. At the time, I remember thinking what a huge waste of time and energy it was. I was feeling strongly like I just wanted to be happy and free, not tied down to someone who had no respect for me.

After several hours, the argument reached a boiling point. We were in the bedroom. I was sitting on the side of the bed and there was a window on the nearby wall. Louis began hitting me. As he delivered punch after punch to my face and chest, I suddenly had a terrifying thought, "He is going to throw me out the window."

Right when I had this thought, Louis blurted out, "I am going to throw you out that [expletive] window!" All I could do was brace myself. In that moment, I thought, "He is about to kill me."

Louis came charging toward me and I was fully prepared for him to pick me up and toss me out the window. He slapped my face and pulled out a clump of hair. Then he delivered a punch to the chest. It was hard enough to send me somersaulting backward off the other side of the bed. I landed under the window. As badly as it hurt, I was relieved not to hear the sound of shattering glass. At that point, I screamed in pain, and through tears I begged him to stop.

Even in the midst of that situation, I believe the Lord ultimately protected my life. There was pain and injury, but God's protection is the only explanation I have for what kept me from being tossed out the window like a limp ragdoll that day.

A while later, the argument finally subsided. On waking the next morning, I was so sore that I could barely move. It seemed like every part of my body was in pain. We had made up before we went to bed, so it was safe for me to tell him that my whole body was in pain. I also told him, yet again, that he better not ever do that to me again. He gave me his best "sincere" apology.

Isolation

In the summer of 1983, my parents called and were extremely excited to tell me that they were planning the celebration of their 50th anniversary, which would take place the following year. I had been in Denver for five years at that point. Dad wanted everyone in the family to be there, so he was prepared to make me a deal. He would pay for my airline ticket that next summer, but the catch was that I had to come home at Christmas and get it from him.

Flying was expensive at that time, so I had not been home often—maybe only three times in the previous five years. Part of me was filled with anticipation and excitement to be with my family, but there was another part of me that quickly developed a sense of dread. Experience had taught me that whenever I left town, I would first endure another episode of beating. Louis's jealousy and insecurity would always surface in the form of accusations: "You're not going there to see your family. You're going there to see your ex-boyfriend!"

As the Christmas of '83 grew closer, I began to brace

myself anytime I was around Louis. I didn't know when the beating would come, but I tried my best to be ready. After a while, I began to wonder . . . *Could it be? Will he let me go without a confrontation and beating?* I began to feel relieved. Happy, even.

Unfortunately, my joy did not last. The night before I was set to leave for Indiana, the arguing began. Louis was true to form. He could not think of any new material. First, he began questioning, "If your parents want to see you, why don't they just come here for Christmas?" Of course, this was not the point. My parents wanted the whole family together to help them plan their anniversary celebration.

It wasn't long before that led to the false accusation that I was actually going to see my ex-boyfriend. The trip had been planned for six months, and Louis had known about it the whole time. There was no rational explanation for this behavior. He just wanted complete control over every aspect of my life.

In the midst of his accusations and anger, I found myself upset that he had waited so long. Why couldn't he have beaten me earlier and just gotten it over with? In between his blows, I screamed through tears that I couldn't believe he was doing this. In reality, I could believe it, but I was angry that he waited so long. He was purposely trying to ruin my time with my family.

The waiting had also gotten my hopes up. Maybe he understands now. Maybe he's different. Maybe he trusts me. It wasn't even my idea to travel there, after all. It was my dad's idea.

All that was left after the fight was to come up with some kind of explanation for my swelling and bruising around my mouth. In a classic, cliché, sort of a way, I composed an incredibly dumb scenario about me clumsily hitting myself in the mouth with a cabinet door.

Fortunately, no one asked about it, but my mother did tell me years later that she had noticed it. There was so much joy and comfort from being in the safety of my family those few days, but at the same time, part of me dreaded going back to Colorado. There were a few times I thought about telling my parents of my predicament, but in the end, I was too ashamed. Our family had no history of violence, so I questioned whether they could possibly understand. I also wasn't sure what they could do to help.

Voluntarily, I returned to my emotional and sometimes physical imprisonment in Denver.

Recognizing Controlling Behavior

You deserve to live according to your beliefs. Often, an abuser will attempt to block anything which limits their control over a victim. Take spiritual beliefs for example. A person's spiritual beliefs are a core part of their identity. They are where we get our moral compass, and we should never be forced to compromise our values.

During my time with Louis, he most often allowed me to go to church. I look back and consider this a godsend—God was getting me to a place where I would no longer want to live the way I was living. I know this was divine providence, because Louis definitely resented the fact that I went to church. Normally, if he didn't like some aspect of my life, he would have moved to shut the door on it.

Combating the Lies: Lie #1—You Don't Have a Voice

We can become voiceless as our self-esteem gets stripped away and we live in a shell. Isolation serves to reinforce this, as we lose meaningful relationships with everyone except our abusers. Often, a woman who is abused has lost her own voice but also the voice of her unborn child. This is part of what leads to coerced abortions. If we won't even speak up or defend ourselves, how can we ever expect to speak up for someone else?

In my own case, I can see that I was losing the ability to stand up for myself even as a child. I had a bully in elementary school who picked on me, and I would not stand up to him. However, God always stands up for the weak, the abused, and the oppressed. We find this over and over in Scripture.

> Learn to do good; seek justice, correct oppression; bring justice to the fatherless, plead the widow's cause.
>
> Isaiah 1:17 ESV

Jesus is the example of how we are supposed to live, and He always stood up for the weak, the oppressed, and the downtrodden. He was never silent about injustice. In perhaps the most meaningful example, Jesus often stood up directly to Satan himself anytime Satan was abusing or oppressing someone.

> And you know that God anointed Jesus of Nazareth with the Holy Spirit and with power. Then Jesus went around

doing good and healing all who were oppressed by the devil, for God was with him.

Acts 10:38 NLT

You have power too. You have the Holy Spirit living inside of you. Jesus Christ has given you authority over the devil, and you do not have to fear him or those who serve the devil.

I have given you authority to trample on snakes and scorpions and to overcome all the power of the enemy; nothing will harm you.

Luke 10:19 NIV

Regardless of our personality, we have to accept responsibility. God has given us a voice, and we must use it. That doesn't mean you run out today and spontaneously confront your abuser without a plan and a support network in place. But it does mean that you get it settled in your heart that you have a God-given voice, and it should not be silenced. You can start using your voice right now by being honest with someone else about what is happening in your life.

Discussion Questions

1. Do you have a history of wanting to stand up for yourself, but remaining silent instead?

2. When did you first begin losing your voice?
3. Where would you say the situation is right now—are you actively standing up for yourself, or are you still being silenced?
4. Is any aspect of your life being blocked or hindered by the person you're in a relationship with?
5. Are you allowed to freely associate with friends, co-workers, and family?
6. Does your partner make you feel guilty for doing normal activities like going to church?

TWO

Broken and Mended

IN JANUARY OF 1987, I began the new year with that wistful hope we often have for new beginnings; a time to shake off the past and move forward with a fresh start. I took some time to pause and reflect over the previous year, and to set some new goals for myself. For some reason, I had a lot more anticipation than normal for new and exciting things that year. I'm not really sure why. It was just a feeling that this year was going to be really good.

As I finished my chores one morning, I folded the ironing board and my hand happened to rub across my stomach. To my surprise, I felt a lump. Pulling my jeans down a couple of inches, I was astonished to see a lump about the size of a pecan. I had no idea what it might be, but I immediately made a doctor's appointment.

Sitting alone in my car after seeing the doctor, I was in a state of shock. I was pregnant! Only in the very early stages of pregnancy, my body had given no indication that I was pregnant. So that part alone was a total shock.

However, there was more bad news. Not only was I carrying an unplanned child, but there were complications. At the time of my first abortion, I was not told about the increased risk of complications that comes from having an abortion (Accurate information is still heavily censored, but it is out there. See here for an example: https://www.compasscare.info/health-information/abortion/abortion-risks-and-side-effects/). The lump I had noticed turned out to be a fibroid tumor. The doctor had felt around while examining me and said that there were several other fibroid tumors. I had never heard of such a thing.

Dr. Bradford had explained to me that fibroids were benign tumors that attach themselves to the uterus. Due to the chemical changes in my body because of the pregnancy, these tumors were growing at an astronomical rate. The doctor said there was no way I could carry a growing baby to term with seven or eight rapidly growing tumors in my uterus.

Upon hearing this news, my very first thought was the vow I had made to God after my first abortion: "God, if I ever get pregnant again, I will have the baby no matter what my circumstances are." Pretty quickly, I started wondering what happens when you break a vow to Almighty God. Do you get struck by lightning? I didn't think so, but I certainly didn't want to find out.

As time progressed and my stomach grew larger and larger, the doctor said he didn't see how I was able to stay on my feet. Dr. Bradford told Louis that if I complained of pain, it was not just me being whiny; that this was a serious medical condition. Louis understood that I was in real pain and tried to be supportive of me, but in reality, he was not emotionally supportive at all. Maybe he just wasn't capable of empathy.

By that time, Louis and I had been together for almost eight years. Louis's perspective was that he still "didn't want me bringing a baby into our relationship" at that time. Adding to that stress, there would also be a stack of medical bills to pay.

Besides those issues, a major seed of fear had been planted when the physician told me that I would not be able to carry the baby to term. That meant the baby would likely have to be born prematurely. Premature babies are much more likely to have health problems and complications. So I worried that the baby could be deformed, mentally impaired, or have other special needs. Thoughts of "what if" dominated my mind.

Perhaps the only good thing I could find in my situation at that time was that I had recently begun attending a new church that I really liked. They had some teaching that I had not previously been familiar with: they frequently used scriptures which taught about God's healing power, and more specifically, how He has given that power to us, His followers. I always believed that God can and does heal, but I had never been taught that as believers, we have authority to speak to disease and sickness. Through their teaching and encouragement, I was now learning to put my faith into action, stand firm, and keep my vow to the Lord.

In spite of all the questions which plagued my mind, I was already beginning to love this child. Determined to carry the child to term, my commitment was tested. Still in my first trimester, my stomach grew rapidly, and the tumors got so large that they were preventing the baby from developing properly. They were also blocking my bladder. Twice, I had to visit the emergency room so they could insert a catheter before my bladder became distended or even ruptured. However, I was determined to press through.

The only option for removing the tumors meant that they would also have to take the baby and "terminate" the pregnancy. It also meant a hysterectomy. Being 36 at that time, it was likely this was my last chance to bear children anyway.

As time progressed, two lives hung in the balance. Not only was the baby at risk, but the doctors increasingly warned that my own life was at risk. They continued to try to steer me toward aborting. The situation was mentally and emotionally draining. Even though I was attending church, listening, and learning, I was not getting involved and getting to know people there. So I had no support system in Denver. My family members were all miles away, and I did not tell them about anything that was going on.

I had a few friends who were aware of what was happening, and they all consistently urged me to abort, warning that it was going to cost me my life if I didn't.

Finally, at the end of my first trimester, there didn't seem to be any other option. After a long, tear-filled prayer, I looked up and said, "I'm sorry, God. I can't do this anymore! I am willing to keep my end of the bargain, but where are you, God? Why don't you heal me?"

In my mind, there was no other option. In my mind, it was either go through with the procedure or I die, in which case the baby dies anyway. Laying on the gurney, they began to roll me into the operating room. I was filled with a sense of dread. The time had come.

One last time, I crossed my arms over my stomach, trying to gently caress the little life inside of me. Fighting back tears, I asked the child to forgive me. Then I prayed it would not hurt the baby very much.

My thoughts switched to Jesus in the Garden of Gethsemane, crying out, "Father, is there any other way?" I couldn't help but ask that same question.

Why must it end like this? God, please forgive me for what I am about to do—taking the life of an innocent one.

The intern took my arms and laid them at my sides, and they began to administer anesthesia. When I woke up, my hysterectomy was over, and I felt like my life was over too. No children. No chance of grandchildren.

A broken vow.

A crushed spirit.

A shattered life.

One thing I knew for sure from that day forward was that no matter what else happened to me in life, I had already lived out the worse day of my life.

The Spirit of Control

Right before the surgery, I told my family that I had fibroid tumors, the removal of which required me to have a hysterectomy. I did not tell them I was pregnant. They decided to come visit and help care for me after the surgery.

Back then, I spent most of my time at Louis's house when I was not at work, so a lot of my daily belongings were there. Knowing of my family's religious background, Louis and I decided to move all of my stuff back into my apartment before my sisters came. We did not discuss what would happen after they left, but I'm sure he assumed that once my sisters were gone, I would go back to spending most of my time at his place. Otherwise, he would never have agreed to let me take my things.

My sisters stayed for a few days until I regained enough strength to get around on my own. As I thanked them for coming and hugged them bye, I couldn't help but wonder what path my life was about to take. All I knew for sure is that I didn't want to continue my relationship with Louis.

With it already being very rocky, there was no way our relationship was about to handle the stress and strain of a hysterectomy and second abortion. Most importantly, I had also decided I could no longer endure his abusive ways.

Having been with him for almost eight years, I realized that the disrespect he would display toward me, along with his controlling nature, vastly outweighed any good times we had. He used to always tell me that in spite of our hard times, we would hang in there and keep our relationship going. When he would say things like that, I would not speak up. However by this point in time, I had made up my mind. We were miserable. What was the point of continuing that way?

This was my chance to escape. Louis was very controlling, and we both had unhealthy emotional ties, as well as emotionally traumatic bonding, happening in our relationship. Looking back, I see it as nothing short of a miracle that Louis agreed to let me stay at my own apartment after surgery. Besides that, I had left my job at the radio station about a year prior, so that meant I didn't have to see him at work either.

I told him that I was needing some time alone for a while, and I began to distance myself from him. Over the next several months, he would contact me, and my responses were always the minimum conciliatory responses I could get by with to keep him at bay. In the meantime, I kept attending the new church I liked so much, and I was growing spiritually.

One evening, Louis contacted me and asked if he could come talk to me. I hesitated, feeling like nothing good would come of it. But I had not seen him for quite some time, and I knew that at some point I would have to face him. So I reluctantly consented.

At first, the conversation went well, kind of like old friends catching up on each other's lives. But eventually, the arguments began. I don't recall exactly what we argued about, and there was no physical violence involved. The main thing that stands out in my mind that night was something Louis said.

After a fairly lengthy argument, Louis was getting ready to leave. He angrily stormed toward the door. Then all of a sudden, he turned back around, pointed his finger at me, and said, "But you're different now, because you have the Holy Spirit, don't you?"

I was totally shocked.

The entire time, I had not said a word to him about church, my relationship with God, or anything else along that line. But as it turns out, I didn't have to say it. He could see it. He recognized the difference in me, and he recognized the source of that difference. But here's the most important part: something in Louis recognized that he no longer had control over me. He could see clearly now that Jesus was my

Lord, not him. And once he saw that, the fight was over. He gave up.

Freedom

To this day, I frequently remember that experience and thank God for it. It taught me the power we have as believers when we are fully surrendered to God. The devil recognizes when this takes place, and he has to flee.

> Submit yourselves, then, to God. Resist the devil, and he will flee from you.
>
> James 4:7 NIV

At that time, I had not ever heard the term "soul tie" (which we go over in detail in chapter five). I didn't understand what they were or how they worked. I didn't have any prewritten deliverance prayers. But I did address the lordship issue that was operating in my life. I had gotten out of the sinful situation, and I had begun to put the Lord first in my life. Those simple steps brought freedom from the abusive and controlling relationship that had dominated my life for nine years.

However, total emotional freedom and healing did not come instantly. As with many people, finding complete freedom and healing was a process. There was more effort involved in getting to the other side of the pain and experiencing wholeness, peace, and fullness of joy in the Lord.

Women Often Suffer in Isolation

One of the major challenges I had in that regard was that I had lived a life of secrecy and isolation. I did not stay close with my family after moving to Denver, and I hid my life choices from them. For the first 7 years or so, Louis and I hid our relationship from our employer, which made it difficult for me to have any real friendships with my co-workers. But I wasn't just hiding from them. I was also trying to hide from Louis while at work.

One time at the very beginning of our relationship, I was talking to a male co-worker in the hallway and I reached out my hand toward him in a normal, friendly kind of gesture. Louis happened to be coming up the stairs at that moment, and saw us talking. Louis later told me that he "saw me flirting" with this other man.

I remember thinking to myself that I had not been flirting. Something in me told me that his reaction wasn't right—that this was a red flag—but I greatly underestimated how serious it was. Still, it was things like that which made me have to constantly hide or live in fear of Louis's retribution for all those years.

There was another occasion when I called my mother and talked to her for a while. After we got off the phone, Louis commented, "You are tied to her apron strings." If that were really the case, would I have moved 1200 miles away from her? Now I know that all of Louis's comments and scoldings were designed to isolate me from others.

There was another incident when a friend called to tell me that she had been in a car accident. She wasn't badly hurt, but she was shaken up and wanting someone to talk with.

After we got off the phone, I looked at Louis and said simply, "Mary was in an accident."

He roared at me, "Who cares!?!"

I did. She was a friend. Of course I cared about what happened to her. But his remarks made me question my own thoughts and even the feelings of concern I felt for her. An abuser feels threatened by his victim having any closeness or concern about anyone else. The spirit of control wants to be *the only* significant relationship in the victim's life.

As with most women, the dominating, controlling spirit was very effective at reaching its goal. Spending my days at work—where I couldn't have friends—and spending all of my free time with Louis, there really was no chance of developing significant relationships with anyone else. If he ever saw that I was starting to associate with someone to the point of it becoming a friendship, he would quickly find ways to thwart the relationship. In his mind, other relationships weren't necessary for me. He was all I needed.

For much of our relationship, I attended church on Sunday mornings, but made very few acquaintances. No one there had any idea of the secrets I kept inside, or the isolation I was living in. Sadly, this is the case much too often with women sitting in our churches. We simply don't know the giants they are facing behind closed doors. To make matters worse, the topics of domestic violence and abortion are rarely ever addressed from the pulpit. When we ignore these topics, it only leads to further isolation and secrecy for women who are suffering.

Carrying the secrecy of abortion only alienates a woman and forces her into further isolation. With isolation being a big piece of the puzzle in domestic violence situations, we are truly putting women at risk by allowing them to exist in isolation. The woman who is hurting only increases her pain. It takes a lot of energy and a huge emotional toll to constantly keep up the facade of a smiling face when you're actually carrying intense pain on the inside. As much trauma as the abortion itself brings, the years that follow intensify the pain if the woman remains shrouded in secrecy, isolation, and shame.

My Healing Journey

Each person travels the path of healing on their own timeline. My healing really started one day when I was browsing at a Christian bookstore. I happened to notice a book titled *Abortion's Second Victim*, by Pam Koerbel. Originally published in 1986, the book was still fairly new at that time, but it is now out of print. The book description said something about emotional healing for women after abortion. I looked at it and thought to myself, *I've had an abortion, but I'm okay*. Looking back today, I can see clearly that nothing was further from the truth. I was not okay, but I was in denial and repression.

In spite of that thought, I took the book straight up to the checkout line. Normally I would browse through a book a good bit before deciding to buy, but for some reason, I didn't this time.

This was right at the beginning of a long Fourth of July weekend. It was a beautiful, sunny Colorado day, so I put on my swimsuit, grabbed my new book, and ran downstairs to the apartment complex pool. After splashing some water on myself, I settled in on a lounge chair and began reading. Tears began to flow as soon as I started the Introduction.

I hadn't even made it to chapter one without crying! Surely the Lord must have protected me from reading through any of it in the bookstore so that I wouldn't look like a blubbering basketcase.

As I read, I had the sense that this author knew everything about me. She understood feelings in me that I had buried, repressed, or denied. Pretty quickly, I closed the book and went back up to my apartment. I didn't understand what was happening, but I knew I needed to read this book behind closed doors, from the safety of my couch.

I opened the book and managed to sob my way through the first few pages. At times, the tears were so dense that I could barely see to be able to keep reading. It was like trying to drive through a blinding rainstorm. My well-kept secrets were being exposed. My abortions had hurt me, and there was no denying it. The painful reality of what I had done, and the damage that was inflicted on my soul, began to sink in. I had to stop reading.

Although I had stopped for the day, I found courage to read more the next day, and that pattern continued. Some days, I could only read one page. Other days, I could make it through several pages. Somedays, it was like I could only take a small bite, whereas other days I could handle a whole meal.

Whatever portion I managed to digest on a given day, I was grateful for it because I could tell that I was slowly beginning to change. I began to feel better. My heart was healing. This Christian author used Scripture and words of wisdom to touch my soul. Nothing heals like the Lord and His Word.

Only taking small portions at a time, the process of finishing the book took three or four months. Daily, I sat at the feet of my Savior, soaking up His goodness through the words of this book, and becoming a different person in the process.

After I finished the book, I visited a church to listen to a guest speaker. Since it was a mid-week service, there were no bulletins. However, after I chose a pew and sat down, I noticed that someone had left their Sunday bulletin in a slot on the back of the pew in front of me. As I waited for the service to start, I perused the bulletin and an announcement caught my eye.

There was a small group for post-abortive women in need of healing. The words on the page seemed so foreign to me. I think I was in shock that anything like this existed. But it felt like a personal invitation directly from God to me.

As soon as I got home, I called the number listed in the announcement. A couple of weeks later, the group started up and I let the Lord do His work of healing in me. Emotions ran the gambit, not just for me, but for all of the participating women. Letting go of our secrets and sharing our stories was a first for most of us. We became a close-knit group as we ventured through our healing process, experiencing the stages of grief, sharing our feelings, confessing our secrets, and praying for each other. It was a safe place, the first one in a very long time for me. Feeling safe was a big deal for all of the women in the group, but especially those of us who had lived through abusive situations.

Shortly after the group study was completed, I began volunteering at a local crisis pregnancy center. Doors opened for me to share my testimony in schools and churches. Wherever I could, I looked for opportunities to encourage other post-abortive women that they could find healing in the Lord.

Around that same time, in 1989, my father had a heart attack and stroke. He stayed in the ICU for about six weeks, and then passed away. I was always a daddy's girl, but since I was still in Colorado at that time, I couldn't be near him the way I wanted to. He had been in good health prior to the stroke, so the whole thing was unexpected. By that point, I had learned a good deal about grief in my Bible study. I understood that everyone's grief process can look and feel different, even though we often seem to share generally recognizable phases. All I knew for sure is that with his passing, there was a great deal of inner turmoil for me. A struggle was taking place that I didn't understand.

My mentor at the crisis pregnancy center reminded me that many post-abortive women take the death of a loved one very hard because they have never resolved the death that occurred during their abortion. Instantly, I understood that this was what I was experiencing. I recognized that I had mourned the death of my second child while going through the abortion recovery group. That was the one that I thought about the most because I had wanted to keep the baby, but couldn't. I felt the most grief and trauma from that second abortion, but I really had not even acknowledged the first abortion yet. The trauma of it was still with me.

So I began the grief process for my first baby, working through all of the guilt, shame, and pain associated with my first abortion. The process brought healing, release, and closure to this part of my life.

Comforting Others with the Comfort I Received

Several months later, I developed an abortion recovery support group in my church. I also led several Bible studies for abortion recovery through the crisis pregnancy center. Shortly after that, I began facilitating a group at church for battered women. Since domestic violence had played a major role in my life, I wanted to help other women who were dealing with that issue.

At that time, I did not understand that there was a larger connection between domestic violence and abortion. However, I began to notice that a lot of the women who were in the abortion recovery group also joined the group for battered women. Doing some research, I found that there is a strong, well-documented connection between domestic violence and abortion,[1] that many women are coerced into abortion by abusive partners,[2] and that the vast majority of women who have abortions report feeling pressured by others to do so.[3]

Leading these groups helped further and solidify my own healing process. One learns a lot by teaching others. A major thing I realized during that time was that God opens doors for us to heal. Whenever He opened one, it was my job to walk through it. As I continued to share this journey with other women, the Lord continued His healing process in my life.

As time went on, I became a member of Operation Outcry, a group for men and women who speak openly about the effects that abortion has had on their lives. I also joined the Silent No More campaign. Healing and helping other women heal began to develop into a full-blown calling for me.

The years progressed, and I attended other abortion recovery programs and weekend retreats—programs like Silent Voices, Ramah, and Deeper Still. There was a drive for me to learn as much as I could so that I could help as many women as possible. I was also driven to continue exploring and participating in these programs, because I would often find that there was some other hidden area of my heart that needed to be healed. I wouldn't even be aware of it until God shined light on it, but I learned over time to just keep going and stay open to whatever He wanted to deal with in me.

At the same time I was getting involved with more and more abortion recovery programs, I was also taking classes and learning as much as possible about domestic violence.

So what is the answer to breaking free? I would say that the first step is just to expose the secret to the light of God's Word. Doing that will allow the warm light of Jesus' love to begin to heal you. Nothing good grows in the dark. As the saying goes, "We are only as sick as our secrets." Being honest with ourselves and others can often seem difficult, but once the secret is exposed, we are able to grieve and healing begins.

Combating the Lies: Lie #2—You Cannot Tell Anyone Your Secrets

This is perhaps the most insidious lie of the enemy. He knows that if he can get you to keep your sin a secret, he can keep you from being healed of it. Abortion is a terrible sin, and it's one that most women are very ashamed to talk about. But when you don't tell anyone else, you carry the memory of your abortion around deep inside of you.

Secrecy will keep us mired in guilt, shame, and torment. We may try to cope by repressing the memory of what happened. We attempt to deny our feelings rather than confronting them. All of this is the emotional equivalent of drinking a dose of poison each day. It may not kill us all at once, but it is definitely making us sick, and if it goes on long enough, it can lead to destruction.

However, God has a very simple remedy!

> Therefore confess your sins to each other and pray for each other so that you may be healed. The prayer of a righteous person is powerful and effective.
>
> James 5:16 NIV

You don't have to tell everyone your sin, but you have to tell someone. If you are reading this in a study group, break up right now into groups of two. Get alone and talk to each other. Confess your sins to your prayer partner and let them pray for you to be healed.

Discussion Questions

1. Do you struggle to believe God can forgive you for your abortion?

2. Are domestic violence and abortion addressed in your church?
3. Freedom and healing are available to you, but you have to be willing to do the work. We have to be willing to face the pain, deal with the issue, and let God heal us. Are you willing?

THREE

Jill's Story

JILL IS AN ADORABLE, petite lady with light brown, shoulder-length hair and sparkling green eyes. At least that's how I know her. But she wasn't always this way.

At the age of 17, she moved out of her home after finding the courage to tell her mother what had happened. Jill's stepfather, Joe, a man she barely knew and had never liked, had tried to molest her. Unfortunately, her mother did not believe her, or at least that's what she said. Sometimes mothers choose to ignore such realities because they simply don't want to deal with it.

In an effort to cry out for help, Jill turned to her grandmother but the outcome was the same. Feeling betrayed by both of these women, Jill moved in with her biological father. This was not a great option, and her father basically neglected her. He was too busy with his own life of going to clubs and dating a carousel of women.

Feeling like she had nowhere to turn, Jill was in survival

mode. She took a job waiting tables at a hole-in-the-wall restaurant called Tiny Tim's Diner. She juggled plates while trying to juggle life, keep up with her homework, her extracurricular activities, and finish her high school education. Living with her father was miserable, but still better than the alternative of going back to her mother and Joe. After a while, Jill was able to scrape together some meager savings and get a place of her own.

Having only a tattered couch and a lumpy old comforter, she secured a cramped studio apartment and began her life as an adult. Finally, she could have some peace and quiet, along with a sense of safety and well-being.

One of Jill's favorite things to do was play the snare drum in her high school band. She also felt like her band director, Mr. Canigglio, was very approachable. The thought occurred to her that he might be able to help her. One crisp autumn afternoon, she asked if she could talk to him for a few minutes after they finished practicing their drills, so he gently took her aside to a quiet place on the football field.

With tears in her eyes, she told him that she would no longer be able to be in the marching band. With a disappointed and puzzled look, he asked why. She explained that she lived alone, worked full-time hours at her job, and was finding it difficult to keep up with her studies. On top of that, she did not have money for the band uniform. Mr. Canigglio said he was sorry to hear of her troubles, and wished her well.

That was strike three.

"Why doesn't anyone help me? Why doesn't anyone care about my situation?" Jill wondered. No one seemed to think she was worthy of a decent, normal life. Everywhere she looked, Jill saw other kids who seemed to be completely carefree, having fun, and enjoying life without being burdened by the kinds of troubles she had experienced. Although she had faced many obstacles in her young life, and had tried her best to overcome them, she was starting to feel defeated.

It was like the instrument she loved to play, the snare, was a metaphor for her life. It seemed to be full of tricks and traps set by an enemy—an enemy who wanted nothing more than to beat her spirit down into submission and hopelessness.

Beyond High School

Jill eventually dropped out of high school. In light of the insecurities and dysfunction she had experienced, she had no specific plan for success and no real goals for her life. Wanting a fresh start, she decided to leave the Midwest since she did not have many good memories there. Jill decided on Virginia Beach as the location for her fresh start. The beach seemed inviting, and would certainly be more exciting than the cornfields where she'd grown up.

Jill arrived at her destination not knowing anyone, but already accustomed to being on her own. She quickly found a job at a popular beer bar. It was legal at that time for 18-year-olds to drink or serve alcohol in Virginia. Jill enjoyed her time at the beach, especially when she met Ryan and fell in love.

Ryan was living at home with his parents at the time, and they invited her to move in. They did not need to ask Jill twice. She longed for stability and family connection, and this situation seemed to provide both. Eventually, she and Ryan got married and moved into their own place.

One afternoon, Jill was at home unexpectedly when Ryan came in with his girlfriend. A heated exchange took place, and Ryan responded by locking Jill in the bedroom so that he could talk to his girlfriend privately. Jill escaped through the window and went to his parents' house. After telling them about what had happened, they went back with Jill to help her get her stuff.

Jill grabbed what few belongings she had, and with an attitude of determined defiance, removed her wedding ring and left it on the dresser before walking out.

Moving On ... From Bad to Worse

After that episode, Jill decided she had enough of life in Virginia and went to live with her Aunt Jane in North Carolina. Soon after she had moved in there, she realized that she was pregnant with Ryan's baby. Jill decided there was no way she was going back to Ryan, so she decided to return to her hometown instead. At that point, she resumed a relationship with Tony, a former boyfriend.

Jill miscarried the baby shortly after returning to her hometown. After the miscarriage, she continued to date Tony, who found pleasure in drugs and always became violent when he was using. Their arguments were frequently physical, and Jill, with her small stature, was no match for Tony. He would chase her threatening to kill her, and Jill would do her best to find a place to hide.

The bathroom was her favorite place to hide. If she could

only get there before he did, she could go in, lock the door, and then brace her legs up against it as she sat against the bathtub. Having been a dancer since the time she was young, Jill's legs were strong, so this made her method very effective. She would often have to sit this way for hours at a time, calling out for help through the bathroom window until she was hoarse. This would go on until Tony finally regained his senses.

Roughly six months after the miscarriage, Jill became pregnant with Tony's baby. He wanted nothing to do with any baby, so his immediate response was to demand an abortion. In fact, when she resisted his demand, he came right out and added this threat: "You will have an abortion, or I will kill you."

Jill did not want an abortion, but she felt she had no choice. She was too frightened to leave Tony. Feeling completely trapped, she went into survival mode. Tony had told her that if she ever left, he would find her and kill her, so any thought of leaving was quickly dismissed. The situation left her feeling hopeless, and the danger only got worse.

Fortunately, Jill was able to confide in one of her aunts, who promptly staged an intervention. Jill was in no shape mentally or emotionally to leave on her own. Her aunt went to their apartment and moved all of Jill's things out while Tony was at work, allowing her to take refuge in her grandmother's basement.

After Jill was gone, Tony decided to make good on his many threats, and systematically began stalking her. One day as she was leaving work, Tony ambushed her in the parking lot. He began beating her, and she screamed for help. Two men were nearby and they came to her rescue, pulling Tony away and calling the police.

Tony was promptly jailed, and from that time on, he never bothered her again. Jill's theory is that once enough people became aware of his threats and violence, he knew he would not be able to get away with killing her. If she were to disappear, Tony would certainly have been the prime suspect. His desire to avoid prison must have outweighed his desire to get revenge on her for leaving him.

The forced abortion and the demeaning experiences caused Jill to begin to seriously resent and even hate all men. However, at the same time, she bounced through relationships and promiscuity, searching for love, all the while unable to see that sex was simply not bringing about the intimacy and true love she desired.

Desperation

As time went on, she met a man named Richard. Their relationship seemed to be different. More solid. But when she got pregnant again, their relationship took a drastic turn. Richard had been telling Jill that he wanted a family and was ready to settle down.

Now that she had gotten pregnant, his story changed. He wasn't ready at all for a baby. He was too young to start a family. They couldn't afford it. The timing was not right. And neither of them was ready for the responsibility, according to Richard. To prove his point, he broke off the relationship, and Jill was left devastated.

Yet again, she was alone and very frightened. Not knowing what to do or where to turn, she rented another studio apartment, having the same assets to her name as the last time—a few clothes, a tattered couch, and that same frayed comforter she had when she first moved out of her parents home. The glaring difference, of course, was that this time she was pregnant. She moved in with only a jar of change left for food.

Jill continued to work, all the while trying to figure out what to do with her life. To her disbelief, she was actually robbed one day while she was at work. The intruders had left her clothes, but they had taken her comforter and her jar of change. What a blow.

Totally desperate at this point, she found her way to a Catholic services agency. For the first time in her life, Jill found someone who cared. They listened to her story and more importantly, they were willing to offer tangible help. A kindhearted lady named Elaine took charge of her case there.

One of the first things Elaine did was urge Jill to move away from the neighborhood she was in, as it was not safe at all, especially for a single expectant mother. Jill countered that this was not an option, as it was the only place she could afford.

Things Begin to Look Up

To Jill's surprise, Elaine told her that her boyfriend had an extra room in his house. Jill could stay with him for a while, rent-free. It sounded good in a way, but at the same time, Jill was hesitant. She had grown to completely distrust men, so moving in with a total stranger ignited all of her worst fears. Would he abuse her? Would he attack her?

As the conversation continued, Jill could tell that Elaine herself was trustworthy. She was full of compassion; a good person. Jill did not trust the boyfriend, but she did trust that Elaine would not put her in any kind of danger. Eventually, she took the offer.

The new living situation turned out to be an absolute Godsend. Evan was the first man Jill had ever met in her life that was truly trustworthy. He was very loving, but in a completely non-sexual way. For the first time in her life, a male was treating her with dignity and respect.

Jill closely watched Evan and Elaine's relationship, and she began to see that there is such a thing as true love. As an added bonus to the situation, it turned out that Evan was the facilitator at Men for Non-Violence, an agency which helped abusive men turn away from their destructive patterns. Jill was learning a lot from Evan and Elaine.

After nine months, Jill gave birth to a healthy baby girl, who she named Jennifer, but called "Jenny" for short. Jill had support from Evan and Elaine, which was incredibly helpful. Richard's mother had also kept in touch with Jill and was helping with diapers and baby food. Richard's mother also really wanted to be part of Jenny's life, and Jill agreed to let her see Jenny from time to time.

However, Jill was very surprised when Richard contacted her the day after Jenny's six-week check-up. He wanted to see the baby. Jill agreed, and quickly found out that Richard had an ulterior motive. He actually wanted to reconcile with Jill and try to make their relationship work. Like most single mothers, Jill dreamed of having a complete family, with a responsible, loving husband and father at home. She wanted to jump at the chance for this dream to become a reality.

However, she decided to use wisdom and take things slowly with Richard. She had been very hurt when he decided to leave her alone and pregnant. Richard would definitely have to earn her trust.

Over the next five months, Richard did that very thing. He and Jill kept talking, and she decided that he was the man she wanted to spend her life with. They married when Jenny was about six months old, and nine months later, they had a son named Bradley. However, their road would not be a smooth one. As it often does, life presented a series of challenges to their young family.

First, Richard's job required frequent transfers, so they often bounced around from state to state. This added a lot of stress to their new marriage, especially with two young children in tow. Eventually, Richard's job landed the family in Florida.

Unfortunately, their marriage problems were both numerous and serious. Richard and Jill managed to stay together for almost a decade, but by the time Jenny was entering third grade, they had decided it was not going to work. Richard moved out, taking Bradley, and went back to his home state of Indiana.

Jill and Jenny eventually went back to Indiana as well. Jill's sister-in-law Pam was in the process of getting a divorce from Jill's brother, Mark. Pam invited Jill and Jenny to live with her until they could get on their feet. It was a great fit. Pam and Jill got along very well, and Pam had children for Jenny to play with.

Pam was a Christian. Shortly after Jill and Jenny moved in, she explained to Jill that she was believing God to reconcile her and Mark, even though they were in the middle of divorce proceedings at the time. Jill had never heard of anything like this. As much as she loved Pam, she began to wonder if maybe she was a little bit off the deep end.

However, as Pam continued to pray and believe God for reconciliation, Jill watched as her situation began to turn around. Mark's heart began to soften, and before long, he and Pam were reunited. Shortly after their divorce was final, they reconciled and got remarried. Jill was completely amazed.

When she attended Pam and Mark's wedding, she was very impressed by the friendly people in the church, especially Pastor Ron. He seemed wise and kind. She liked the people so much that she began attending the Sunday morning services regularly. As Jill learned more and more about a God who loved her, she frequently found herself at the altar, praying and asking Him for help with her life.

Jill was now 37 years of age. Twenty years had passed since she had moved out of her mom and stepdad's house at the age of 17. Jill noticed that her desires began to change. She had always loved heavy metal music, but now she found herself wanting to listen to Christian radio.

One day on her way home, she tuned in to a broadcast from Focus on the Family. The featured guest ended his time that day by saying that the most important thing in life is to be born again and have a relationship with the living God. Jill knew what those words meant. She had learned about it from the church services and Pastor Ron's teaching.

Suddenly, as the guest said those words, Jill had an "aha" moment. She realized she had been praying to God about all kinds of things, but she had not been born again. "I have never asked Jesus to come and live in me. I have not given my life to Him and been born again. That's what I need to do!"

She quickly pulled into a nearby convenience store, and right there in the parking lot, she repeated the prayer that the guest had outlined for listeners. With that, she drove away as a new woman—a new creation in Christ, as described in 2 Corinthians 5:17. From that time on, Jill and Richard began a process of reconciliation. Their divorce was never finalized, and they have now been married for 38 years.

A New Start

In the early days after beginning a relationship with the Lord, Jill began learning that God wants to heal us of our hurts from the past. Eventually, she began to think about the abortion experience. When it first came to mind, she would quickly try to suppress any thoughts about it. But as time went on, she started thinking that perhaps it made more sense to go ahead and try to deal with it. There did seem to be some issues there and she realized she needed healing.

The next January, she went to a march organized by Right to Life, the nation's oldest pro-life organization. While there, she heard testimonies of women who were involved with the Silent No More campaign—a national campaign whereby Christians make the public aware of the devastation abortion brings to women and men. The women explained how they had received the emotional and spiritual healing they needed after joining a Bible study for women who had previously had an abortion.

Several weeks later, she heard of a guest speaker who was coming to a local church. The speaker was a lady who shared candidly about her experience with abortion and how important it was for women to experience God's forgiveness and healing. Jill decided it would be wise for her to go to this meeting, and as she listened, tears rolled down her face.

Jill knew that the pain had to come out.

She could identify with many emotions and feelings the lady talked about, and this helped Jill realize that she wasn't "crazy" for feeling this way. She also realized she wasn't alone. Depression, shame, low self-esteem, mood swings, and numbness are a few of the symptoms experienced by many women after an abortion.

About a year after seeing the lady speak about these issues, Jill found a Bible study called "Forgiven and Set Free" which was being held at a local crisis pregnancy center. The Lord honored Jill's efforts as she spent time doing her lessons. She began to feel like a weight was being lifted off of her. The more she shared with others in a safe setting, the more she was being healed emotionally.

A couple of years after that, Jill heard about a weekend retreat for women who needed to experience recovery and healing from their past abortions. The retreat was put on by Deeper Still, a ministry which helps women find lasting freedom and healing from abortion. Even though there had been some measure of healing in Jill's life from the Bible study and her relationship with God, she still did not feel completely free, so she made the decision to attend.

The retreat not only dealt with abortion, but other relevant issues surrounding the experience. At the retreat, Jill worked through issues like strongholds that develop, soul ties, worthiness, and relationships. She developed a deeper understanding of Christ's sacrifice for her on the cross and even had a beautiful memorial service for her child, which allowed Jill to go through a healthy grieving process. The retreat was so valuable for her that she later became part of the team for Deeper Still, and she now works to help other women recover from abortion.

It has been a long road for Jill, but her testimony never ceases to amaze me. God took the life of a wandering 17-year-old and brought it to stability and servanthood. He is truly a God of healing and restoration!

Do You Need a New Start?

Jesus stands ready and willing to give you a new start today. If you don't know Jesus as your Lord and Savior, you can give your life to Him right now. Understand that Jesus died a gruesome death on a cross for you. He took your sins upon Himself so that you could receive complete forgiveness and become part of His family. If you would like to do that right now, please pray this prayer:

> *God,*
>
> *I recognize that I have sinned, and I need a Savior. I ask You to forgive me of all of my sins, and I receive Jesus as my Lord and Savior. I give my life to you. Thank you for making me part of your family. In Jesus' name, amen.*

Combating the Lies: Lie #3—You Cannot Let Others In

When a woman's heart has been wounded by abortion, she often spends years suffering in isolation. The same is true for a woman suffering in an abusive situation. Either way, isolation is one of the most toxic and dangerous traps we fall into.

When a woman remains isolated, she is essentially shutting out all voices of reason and truth. The Bible warns us about this danger:

> Whoever isolates himself seeks his own desire; he breaks out against all sound judgment.
>
> Proverbs 18:1 ESV

The Bible also gives us the remedy:

> And let us not neglect our meeting together, as some people do, but encourage one another, especially now that the day of his return is drawing near.
>
> Hebrews 10:25 NLT

> Yes, there are many parts, but only one body. The eye can never say to the hand, "I don't need you." The head can't say to the feet, "I don't need you."
>
> 1 Corinthians 12:20-21 NLT

Just to give you a practical example, I once told a friend

that Louis said he was always right. My friend laughed out loud, and at first, I was puzzled by his reaction. After thinking about it for a while, I realized that my friend's laughter opened my eyes to what a ridiculous statement this was. No one is always right. But I had lived for years as though the statement was true. I had been programmed not to question Louis or his decisions.

The bottom line is that we need to connect and communicate with others who are themselves healthy and have our best interests in mind.

Although Jill had a long journey out of her pain, she did come out of the pain, and it's important to note how the process started. There was the steady downward spiral of difficulties, but you might have also noticed the slow steady stream of rejection Jill experienced. Over and over in her life, she experienced rejection from people she was reaching out to for love. This wore on her self-esteem.

Often, women are only open to the idea of abortion after they have been psychologically aborted themselves. Jill was still a young girl when she experienced molestation by her stepfather, and then rejection by her mother, her grandmother, and even Mr. Canigglio.

The messages of rejection that Jill received caused her to believe she was not worthy of help. She began to shut out anyone who might actually treat her well or help her in some way.

The pattern of rejection continued with the men she dated. Domestic violence reinforced the message of rejection. It was communicated to Jill over and over in her life that she was not worthy of respect, dignity, love, or a healthy life.

What does it mean to be psychologically aborted? One definition might be when a person has been rejected, betrayed, minimized, or made to feel unworthy. These are abortions of the soul, with the soul being defined as our "mind, will, and emotions."

Discussion Questions

1. Can you recognize any patterns of rejection in your own life?
2. What is the first time you can remember experiencing an abortion of your soul?
3. Have you been the victim of domestic violence?
4. If so, are you ready to go on a journey of forgiveness and healing?

FOUR

The Dynamics of Domestic Violence

WHY?

Have you ever wondered why any man would abuse the woman he's supposed to love and care for? Have you ever tried to dissect the reasons why a woman would continue to stay in that cycle? We've all seen it happen. Many of us have experienced it. But do we really understand it?

The "good news"—if we can use that term—is that it is possible to understand what drives the cycle of domestic violence. And that understanding can help those who are seeking to break the cycle, either for themselves or someone else.

First, let's explore what we mean by the term "domestic violence." One good definition might be, "a pattern of purposeful, deliberate, and systematic abusive behavior which is used by the abuser to gain and maintain control over another person." The pattern might include, but is not limited to, intimidation, manipulation, coercion, threats, blaming, humiliation, fear, isolation, and acts that may result in physical injury.

It's obvious to most everyone that kicking, hitting, shoving, slapping, and other forms of physical violence constitute abuse. But there are other forms of abuse.

For example, **mental abuse** might mean playing mental 'games' with a significant other, such as twisting their words, or blaming the victim for the abuser's behavior. Sometimes the abuser will flatly deny things that the victim recalls perfectly, causing the victim to begin to question their own memory and even their sanity. This is sometimes referred to as "crazymaking."

Abusers frequently change the 'rules' of engagement to fit their agenda at that particular moment, resulting in confusion, frustration, and submission for the victim. The victim is also often made to feel like they need to justify their own actions, even though they are the ones frequently being abused and mistreated. All of this is designed by the abuser to slowly chip away at the victim's self-esteem, and diminish their voice.

Emotional abuse (also known as **psychological abuse**) usually refers to direct verbal abuse that targets the victim's emotional state, such as humiliation (either public or private), name calling, insults, mocking, or threats. Emotional abuse also occurs when the victim's phone, computer, or journal is taken and explored by the abuser. The victim's privacy is violated and they are made to feel trapped. The abuser is working to gain control of the victim. Another example is withholding important information from the victim in an attempt to make them feel inferior and subservient, and to try to limit their options for getting away. A prime example would be not having access to important documents such as birth certificates.

Financial abuse occurs when one partner takes control of the finances in a relationship as a means to control and demean the other person. Examples might be when all the money flows through the abuser. The victim has to ask or even beg for money or account for every penny they spend. The victim may not have access to bank accounts, and might even turn over all of their own earnings to the abuser. Credit cards are sometimes taken out in the victim's name and used by the abuser, in an attempt to extort personal gain and simultaneously ruin the victim's creditworthiness, further crippling her financially. The abuser may also force the victim to leave her job in an attempt to further isolate her and deepen her dependence on the abuser.

Verbal abuse includes verbal forms of emotional abuse, as described earlier. But it also includes things like screaming, yelling, vulgarity, swearing, and shouting at the victim in an attempt to harass or terrorize them.

Sexual abuse shows up frequently in domestic violence situations and includes unwanted sexual touching, unwanted sex, coercion, rape, or frequent sex on demand, even though it is not beneficial, healthy, pleasurable, or desirable for the victim. Other examples are forced sex with others and insisting on sexual dress that the victim is not comfortable with. In some cases, an abuser might force a woman to get pregnant against her will through unprotected sex. And in some of those cases, a woman might be forced to get an abortion after she conceives.

Physical abuse includes physical battery, as described earlier. This form of abuse manifests as actions like hitting, punching, slapping, choking, pulling hair, and physically restraining or holding down the victim. Abusers might also throw victims into walls or furniture or use weapons. Basically any type of physical act that brings injury or even death is considered physical abuse.

But it is not limited to those acts. Sometimes physical behavior is used to send messages to the victim. For example, the abuser may throw or break objects near the victim, drive recklessly, destroy items (especially items that are important or meaningful to the victim), or punch walls. Another example is when the abuser harms a pet, either to emotionally harm the victim who has an emotional bond with the pet, or to send a message that "you're next if you don't comply."

When all is said and done, the psychological pain of abuse can do just as much or more damage than physical injury. The old adage that "sticks and stones may break my bones, but words can never hurt me" is not true. Words hurt.

Among people who study the effect of words, there is a common finding that it takes five positive comments to offset one negative comment.[1] Imagine the effect an abuser can have on their victim by making negative comments all day, every day, while never giving any real love or encouragement.

Domestic violence is a learned and repeated behavior. It is sometimes generational. One of my mentors, Debbie Stafford, points out that it is extremely common for children who are raised in domestic violence to repeat those behaviors when they are older. The cycle is often reinforced with drug and alcohol abuse. But just like with drug and alcohol abuse, the cycle of domestic abuse often requires some type of intervention in order to be broken.

According to womenshealth.gov, "A boy who sees his mother being abused is 10 times more likely to abuse his female partner as an adult. A girl who grows up in a home where her father abuses her mother is more than six times as likely to be sexually abused as a girl who grows up in a non-abusive home."[2] Basically, children raised in a violent setting learn that this is what normal behavior looks like. They learn what they have seen, heard, and experienced, and they are highly likely to repeat the behaviors.

Even children in the womb have been shown to be aware of arguments, loud voices, and other trauma. When a pregnant mother is involved in a domestic violence situation, the baby can be born traumatized.[3]

As with abortion, domestic violence does not know any racial, social, or economic boundaries. People of all races, locations, religions, or age groups can experience domestic violence.

Recognizing the Signs

Some behavioral characteristics might be able to help serve as indicators for abusers. Abusers often are able to mask their dysfunction and even appear as "Mr. Nice Guy" to the outside world. In such cases, they often have a dual personality in the vein of Dr. Jekyll and Mr. Hyde. But telltale signs still exist. Recognizing these signs is an important step for anyone who suspects abuse and wants to help. They are also very helpful for women who are dating someone they suspect could have abusive tendencies.

The controlling abuser might be very "now" oriented, pushing for rapid escalation of the relationship. They may also display signs of jealousy early on in the relationship. Abusers can tend to push for exclusive commitment very early in the relationship. Often, battered women date or know their abusers for less than 6 months before taking some major step of commitment such as living together, becoming engaged, or getting married.

Abusers are often skilled at "selling" their behavior to victims. The abuser will often try to justify their jealousy and demands for commitment by saying that these things are a sign of their love and devotion. In reality, they are signs of possessiveness and a lack of trust. Abusers will also claim that many of their control mechanisms are being done for the woman's safety. For example, an abuser may get angry because the woman is late. He may question where she went and who she talked to. If she becomes uncomfortable or expresses reservations about his behavior, the abuser will respond by explaining that all of his behavior is due to his personal concern for the victim and her safety. Louis did this to me early in our relationship, and then would often explain that he "didn't want me to end up being his next big news story."

Abusers will often voice irrational or abnormal fear of being abandoned or experiencing infidelity by the victim. They will also tend to blame others for their personal problems. For example, if they are chronically unemployed, they will tend to blame others at past jobs, claiming that someone is always out to ruin them.

As the relationship progresses, almost anything that goes wrong will somehow end up being the victim's fault. And once the abuse progresses to verbal and physical abuse, the abuser will blame her, essentially arguing that she drove him to do it.

Not to excuse the behavior at all, it's helpful to acknowledge and understand that the abuser himself is often dealing with insecurities and emotional pain. He is out of touch with his emotions, and unable to cope with the normal stresses of life and relationships. The abuser has probably suffered from abuse or neglect in his childhood or teenage years.

The abuser violates others' boundaries. As a result, the victim gradually loses sight of healthy personal boundaries for herself and her children. The abuser never believes that his behavior should have real consequences. A simple apology or rationalization is normally all an abuser is willing to give as a concession.

In fact, serious abusers believe that their domineering and controlling behavior is for the good of the family. They often believe in male supremacy. When violence toward the victim begins to fail to reach the abuser's goal of control, they may turn toward threats or even attempts of suicide to keep the victim trapped. Sadly, the end result of such situations can be suicide or even homicide, without proper intervention.

Cycle of Abuse

Many domestic violence situations go through a predictable cycle. See if any of this sounds familiar.

Things are going smoothly. The couple feels happy, at least as they understand happiness in a relationship. The victim is very compliant, and usually accepts the blame for most problems. While she often feels that this is unfair, she compromises due to her desire to keep things peaceful.

The abuser becomes increasingly agitated. This could be due to disagreements in the relationship, but is usually also driven by things like alcohol and drug abuse, problems at work, or other frustrations the abuser is experiencing outside of the relationship. The abuser starts to express anger and becomes verbally abusive. The victim tries to take a stand for herself, expressing disagreement with the abuser's assertions, demands, justifications, or lines of reasoning.

Tension escalates rapidly, until there is a "blowup" of

anger and violence. At that point, the abuser unleashes the full scope of violence toward the victim. This is known as the "incident phase" or the "acute battering phase."

After the violence has stopped, the partners will find a way to "make up" and re-bond. They may even feel that they have worked out their differences. Both parties welcome this stage, and it is sometimes called the reconciliation phase. Others may call it the "honeymoon stage" or even the "hearts and flowers stage" as the abuser seems loving and remorseful, and may beg forgiveness. He may even bring presents.

Frequently during this stage, abusers will tell victims they are sorry and even promise that they will never do this again. They seem sincere and adamant. The partners forgive and move on from the fight. Unfortunately, the abuser does not make any real attempt to change. All of the gifts and apologies and professions prove to be a manipulative move designed to keep the woman trapped in the relationship.

As time progresses, the cycle repeats itself with the tension building, the breaking point, the abuse, honeymoon phase, and then a calm phase. The steps of this cycle come to define the relationship.

However, the cycle does not merely repeat. They get worse. If couples do not get the help, tools, and skills they need, the cycle will repeat until the couple becomes accustomed to living in very unhealthy and frightening dynamics.

The more a couple repeats the cycle, the more the violence, threats, and aggression will increase. The risk of injury or death becomes higher and higher each time the cycle repeats itself. As the cycle progresses, the honeymoon stage may eventually get eliminated. At this point, the relationship becomes very painful for the abused without having any redeeming qualities. The victim may try to leave, and if the abuser senses that he is losing control, the risk of serious injury or death becomes much higher.

Power and Control Wheel

The Power and Control Wheel is a tool that can help explain the dynamics of abusive situations.

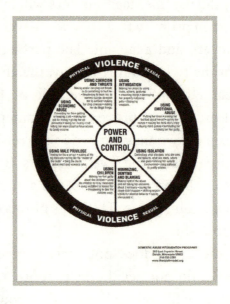

The Power and Control Wheel is used as an indicator of dynamics that are taking place in the abusive situation. Each section of the wheel represents tactics that the perpetrator uses to systematically control their partner. Intimidation, isolation, and various forms of coercion are tools the abuser employs to keep his partner trapped. The print on the graphic is fairly small, so for our purposes, it's helpful to number the sections and list the description of each one:

1. Using Intimidation: Making her afraid by using looks, actions, and gestures. Smashing things. Destroying her property. Abusing pets. Displaying weapons.
2. Using Emotional Abuse: Putting her down. Making her feel bad about herself. Calling her names. Making her think she's crazy. Playing mind games. Humiliating her. Making her feel guilty.
3. Using Isolation: Controlling what she does, who she sees and talks to, what she reads, and where she goes. Limiting her outside involvement. Using jealousy to justify actions.
4. Minimizing, Denying, and Blaming: Making light of the abuse and not taking her concerns about it seriously. Saying the abuse didn't happen. Shifting responsibility for abusive behavior. Saying she caused it.
5. Using Children: Making her feel guilty about the children. Using the children to relay messages. Using visitation to harass her. Threatening to take the children away.
6. Using Male Privilege: Treating her like a servant. Making all the big decisions. Acting like "the master of the castle." Being the one to define men's and women's roles.
7. Using Economic Abuse: Preventing her from getting or keeping a job. Making her ask for money. Giving her an allowance. Taking her

money. Not letting her know about or have access to family income.
8. Using Coercion and Threats: Making and/or carrying out threats to do something to hurt her. Threatening to leave her, to commit suicide, or to report her to welfare. Making her drop charges. Making her do illegal things.

As you can see from reading through the list, abusers are very skilled and persistent when it comes to keeping their victims trapped. If the woman does manage to leave the situation, an abuser may resort to some form of stalking. In the age of social media, stalking is made that much easier. Furthermore, abusers can sometimes track things like cell phones and vehicles. All of this adds to the danger of the situation.

Characteristics of Battered Women

As with abusers, victims are found in all different socioeconomic levels, religions, locations, races, and age groups. However, victims tend to have similar patterns and characteristics. These can be used to help identify when someone you know is being abused, to identify abuses in your own current relationship, or to identify patterns of abuse in your past relationships.

First, it's helpful to understand the mindset of abuse victims. They are often patiently trying to discover a magic formula that will solve the abuse problem in their relationship. She tries to convince her partner of her devotion and loyalty, but it is to no avail, as abusers do not operate on trust. The victim has to constantly be on guard about every move she makes, so as to avoid being accused of wrongdoing by the abuser. Jealous abusers will often accuse victims of flirting, being seductive, or having an affair. So you might notice a woman being extra careful and going out of her way to avoid talking to other men.

Just like the abuser believes his behavior is "for the good" of the relationship and the family, the victim comes to believe that her compliance is for the same reason. She believes that if she can just be compliant enough, and find ways to avoid the punishment of the abuser, everyone will be better off, and that their relationship and family problems will be solved.

However, this is an unreachable goal as it is ultimately impossible to keep an abuser from becoming violent or angry. This leads the victim to experience the feeling of repeated failure.

On the other hand, there are abuse victims who recognize that the abuser is the one who is primarily in the wrong. In those cases, the abuse may be occurring relatively infrequently, such as once every few months. The abuser often swears he will never do it again, and the period of peace gives hope to the victim that he has "really changed" this time. Generally, the less severe and less frequent the abuse is, the more likely the victim is to stay in the situation.

Many abuse victims grew up in abusive homes and have not experienced life without abuse. This type of abuse victim has come to accept abuse and domestic violence as normal behavior. Some victims may not see themselves as battered, or as victims of abuse. In such a case, the victim may have convinced herself that outsiders should never be involved in private marital and family affairs.

Often, women feel economically trapped and do not see any way out. She may view going on welfare as being worse than staying with the abuser. Additionally, she may not have access to any significant amount of cash, and therefore she may feel that she has no option to leave. Abusers also withhold important documents, such as birth certificates and social security cards, to further entrap their victims.

Ultimately, the primary driving motivation for abuse victims to stay in an abusive situation is fear. The victim does not see any way to fully protect herself or her children from the abuser. If she reports him to the police, he can get out on bail and come after her. If the police are contacted by third parties, she will often deny to police that abuse is occurring. Not only does she fear retaliation, but part of her is still trying to prove her loyalty to the abuser. She thinks that if she can prove her loyalty, the abuser will not harm her, so denying the abuse ultimately becomes a survival tactic of sorts for the victim. Embarrassment can be another major reason that victims keep the abuse secret.

As long as the victim is able to keep others out, she is, in a strange way, relieved to keep the situation within her four walls. On one hand, she doesn't like her situation and wants to escape. But because she doesn't feel like that's a viable option, her "solution" is to keep the abuse hidden. She feels that she has learned how to "survive" the situation, as bad as it may be. And fear of the unknown—such as where she will go, how she will live, what will happen to her children—seems worse to her than staying in the current situation.

This all leads the victim to live in isolation. Sadly, the

abuser often becomes her only support system psychologically because he has systematically destroyed or cut off all other relationships. If any friends do hang around for very long, they can often sense that something is wrong. If they sense that something is off about the relationship, they often become uncomfortable and withdraw. They may decide that the abuser is "just a jerk" and not someone they want to hang around with. All of this further exacerbates the problem of isolation.

In both my case and Jill's case, we were miles away from our families and hometowns. We were in a "foreign land," so to speak, where we had no friends, family, or support system.

Abuse victims are often unaware of the many safehouses and other rescue and support systems that exist.

Some abuse victims do seek out help for a time, but then ultimately go back to their abusers. In those cases, family and friends may grow tired of helping. In that sense, a victim can sometimes burn all of her bridges, making her entrapment more severe.

Often a battered woman's inability to act on her own is due to something called "learned helplessness." That term basically means that a woman has effectively "learned" that her behavior has no ultimate effect on the outcome of the situation. She may have tried to leave, threatened to leave, or done everything she could think of to try and change the situation, all to no avail. She feels that she will be abused no matter what she does. She starts to believe what her abuser communicates to her—that she is incompetent and incapable of handling life on her own.

Because the abuser is often violent only with his partner,

the abused partner will tend to conclude that something must be wrong with her. That it must be her fault after all. She may ultimately come to accept his reasoning that she "deserved" the punishment he dealt out.

Some women have beliefs about marriage and men that may lead them to stay in an abusive situation. For example, she may believe that it is ultimately best for children to have a father around, even if he is abusive toward her. She may believe that abuse is part of every marriage, and she may just accept it as part of the "for better or for worse" vow she made. She may view the abuser as a victim himself. For example, if he had an abusive father, she may ultimately want to help or "fix" her abuser from his own pain and tragedy.

As you can imagine, all of these various dynamics can ultimately lead a woman into severe depression. And a severely depressed person is very unlikely to take action.

There are many different dynamics at play in situations of domestic violence that cause victims to become trapped. If you can recognize any of these dynamics in your current relationship, please seek help now.

If you recognize these in someone you know, please consider staging an intervention.

If you recognize these dynamics in a past relationship of your own, the key is to understand how you got trapped so that you avoid it going forward. You should never fall victim to abuse again.

Abuse and the Church

Sadly, many American churches have not handled the issue of domestic violence and abuse very well. The first problem is that pastors are often silent on the issue. Pastors are probably unaware of any abusive situation taking place in their congregation, but as we've just covered, the very nature of domestic abuse keeps it hidden from others. So simply "not being aware" of any abuse does not absolve pastors from their responsibility to address the issue.

When issues of abuse are brought up to ministers and other church staff, they are often dealt with in the form of counseling. A woman trapped in abuse needs rescue and intervention, not a counseling session. However, church staff might only suspect abuse, but without an admission from the victim or the abuser, they may feel that their hands are tied. So what is the solution?

Often, any action at all is better than no action. Confronting the abuser, contacting law enforcement, and staging a rescue and intervention of the victim are all viable options. If we see abuse or suspect abuse but then do nothing, we could ultimately end up with blood on our hands.

One of the most important things the church can do is to help with any physical needs the woman may have. This could range from transportation, finances, medical attention, food, or shelter.

By showing acts of love, mercy, and compassion for the physical needs she has, the church touches the emotional and spiritual part of her. Sometimes just listening will help because she lives in isolation.

The church can also help by referring her to victim assistance funds and programs. She may need help developing a safety plan.

Certainly pray with her. She spends enough time praying alone. Encourage her by giving her biblical hope. Frequently, professional counseling will also be needed.

Encourage her to build a support system around her of family and friends so as not to rely solely on the church. But also remember that she has been isolated, so friends and family may not be readily available. After initial help is given, continue to follow up with her.

Always contact authorities if her life is in danger.

Depending upon the situation, members of the ministry team could go to her house, but there should always be two people at the very least. As a general rule it is best for *an individual* not to try to rescue the abused or get very personally involved. You don't want other vulnerable people, especially women, putting themselves in unnecessary danger. Instead, they can primarily be there for her at a safe distance. If an actual intervention is needed to get her to safety, try to involve professionals and law enforcement.

Help for men who are repentant abusers could include facilitating accountability groups or support groups.

The size of the congregation might determine how involved a particular church wants to be. A large enough church might consider developing a complete ministry team that goes through professional training for this issue. This will allow the church to be better equipped to recognize and respond to abusive situations.

Misuse and Abuse of the Biblical Teaching on Submission

We are all commanded to submit to one another out of reverence for Christ.

> Submit to one another out of reverence for Christ.
>
> Ephesians 5:21 NIV

Right after that verse, wives are told to submit to their husbands as the church submits to Christ, and husbands are told to love their wives as Christ loved the church. So yes, wives are instructed to submit to their husbands, but that instruction comes right after all Christians are told to "submit to one another." So the instruction must be properly viewed in that light.

The instruction for wives to submit to their husbands has been abused by various people in Christian circles. Imagine how an abusive husband who uses religion as a means of control could use this verse to further enslave his victim. It has happened, and it's a real travesty when church leaders go along with or support such an abuser's position.

If the ministry team at a church is going to tell a wife to submit to her husband in everything, they had better make sure that husband is keeping the command to love his wife as Christ loved the church. Christ is not a wife beater. Christ does not enslave. Christ does not abuse authority. Christ does not entrap people and force them to stay under His control.

Christ is a "husband" who operates in love, freedom, and trust. That's who the church submits to, and if a husband can operate with those same characteristics, a godly wife will gladly defer to his loving authority in the home.

Sadly, when there are problems in a marriage, and abuse is present, it often is not addressed properly by ministry teams. She can forgive without remaining in the abusive situation. If she wants to remain married, she can believe God to heal her marriage without staying physically present in the dangerous situation. On the other hand, if her husband abuses her, she does not have to be "trapped" or enslaved by her own marriage vow, when her husband's marriage vow is being broken daily. The Baptist Standard has an excellent article which breaks down the issue:

> God hates divorce, and it is not part of his original design for marriage (Malachi 2:16; Genesis 2:24). Nevertheless, Scripture presents cases where divorce is permissible.
>
> In the New Testament, the two explicit exceptions to the general rule against divorce are adultery (Matthew 5:32; 19:9) and abandonment by an unbelieving spouse (1 Corinthians 7:15). But are these the only exceptions?
>
> Since there is no explicit exception for abuse, many Christians assume abuse must not be legitimate grounds for divorce. But this perspective fails to consider important cultural background information.
>
> Jesus, Paul and most of the earliest Christians were Jewish. As such, we must read the New Testament's teachings on divorce against the backdrop of contemporary Jewish perspectives in order to gain clarity on what the New Testament teaches.
>
> In the *NIV Zondervan Study Bible*, Rikk Watts says: "The Scriptures assume divorce's reality (Deuteronomy 24:1-4),

and all Jews accepted that it was legal; they debated only its grounds. Everyone agreed that adultery and other similarly weighty offenses—e.g., abuse, cruelty, humiliation, persistent refusal to provide requisite food or clothing, willful conjugal or emotional neglect (cf. Exodus 21:10–11) —were clear cause for divorce and required the punishment of the offending party."

Adultery?

In the Gospel of Matthew, Jesus says that a man may not divorce his wife for any cause, but only for adultery (*porneia*).

In Jesus' day, there was a fierce debate between two schools of thought within Judaism—the Shammaites and the Hillelites. The latter read Deuteronomy 24:1-4 as giving a man permission to divorce his wife for pretty much any reason. The Shammaites, on the other hand, argued that "indecency" in Deuteronomy 24:1-4 only meant adultery.

However, both schools of thought affirmed that a woman being neglected or abused by her husband had the right to receive a divorce, and Jewish courts could go so far as to beat the neglectful and/or abusive husband until he agreed to give his wife a certificate of divorce, thus legally freeing her to remarry.

When Jesus says a man may divorce his wife only for *porneia*, he is not providing a comprehensive manifesto on divorce and remarriage; he is addressing a specific intramural Jewish debate of his day. On the question of "any cause divorce," Jesus sides with Shammai.

In Jewish culture in Jesus' time, women could not initiate divorce and had virtually no legal recourse to protect themselves from being divorced. Divorce typically brought shame on a woman and left her economically vulnerable. Jesus' command actually served to protect women from selfish husbands who sought to throw away their wives like trash.

Jesus, however, says nothing about Exodus 21:10-11 or Jewish interpretation of that passage, giving us no explicit evidence he interpreted the text differently or sought to overturn its teaching.[4]

Joshua Sharp, The Baptist Standard

Legalistic interpretations of single verses often ignore the glaring reality of many other relevant Scriptures. Telling a wife that she cannot divorce a man who hits her, beats her, screams at her, or engages in other serious forms of abuse is possibly the height of religious legalism. We're talking about forcing one specific person to follow the letter of one specific rule while completely ignoring everyone else's much more weighty scriptural requirements of love and protection of the innocent, not to mention gentleness and peace. Indeed, a pastor or ministry team who tells an abused woman that she must remain with her abusive husband is tying up a heavy, cumbersome load on this poor woman while themselves not lifting a finger to help.

They tie up heavy, cumbersome loads and put them on other people's shoulders, but they themselves are not willing to lift a finger to move them. (Matthew 23:4 NIV)

The New Living Translation states that same verse this way:

> They crush people with unbearable religious demands and never lift a finger to ease the burden.
>
> Matthew 23:4 NLT

Telling an abused woman to remain with her husband because "divorce is not permitted" is putting an unbearable religious demand on her.

Other times, the woman's own religious background may cause her to feel that it is her "duty" to endure her abusive husband. He may claim that the violence will stop if she simply "submits." If he is explicitly an unbeliever, she may think that by "submitting" she will win him to the Lord.

What we must understand is that Ephesians 5:22 is an instruction to wives given in the context of mutual love and respect between a Christian husband and wife. When a husband is doing his best to love his wife as Christ loved the church, she can and should do her best to submit to him *in the same way all Christians are told to submit to one another.* That is, by thinking of his needs above her own self-centered desires. She can then be a wonderful helpmate to him as the Lord intends. Of course, this assumes that he is also fulfilling his obligation to love her as Christ loved the church, indeed laying down his own life for her.

> Husbands, love your wives, just as Christ loved the church and gave himself up for her.

Ephesians 5:25 NIV

The bottom line is that a woman needs to feel like her husband will do anything in the world to protect her, and we see this reflected in God's command in verse 25. God's design is that a wife should feel perfectly safe and protected with her husband, and that is the context of this passage. Men need to feel honored and respected, and that is another major point of this passage.

The point of the passage in Ephesians is *not at all* for abused women to remain enslaved by their abusive husbands. That is not what God is saying here!

When the Abusive Husband "Repents"

One issue that comes up in church and counseling environments is what to do when the abusive husband seems repentant. Jesus gives Peter a relevant instruction about forgiving his neighbor who sins against him.

> Jesus answered, "I tell you, not seven times, but seventy-seven times."
>
> Matthew 18:22 NIV

Just for purposes of illustration, note that a religiously legalistic interpretation of that verse might involve counting the number of offenses and stopping the forgiveness at number 78. However, as a practical matter, we know good and well that isn't what Jesus was communicating when He said this.

Instead, He seems to be pointing toward the fact that He is willing to forgive us without limit, and we should be willing to do the same. But forgiveness does not in any way imply that we must continue to subject ourselves to the same offenses over and over.

Let's take a practical example. Say you have a neighbor who borrows your lawnmower, but he is careless with it and breaks it. The lawnmower was expensive. It has value to you and your family. But the neighbor is very sorry and asks your forgiveness. Sometime later, after you've bought a new lawnmower, the neighbor asks you to borrow the new one. Are you required by Jesus to say yes? What if he does this over and over? Are you required to keep saying yes, keep forgiving, and keep holding onto the hope that one day your neighbor will learn not to be so careless, self-centered, and foolish?

You could take a legalistic interpretation of certain verses and come up with an answer of "Yes." But as a practical matter, we know that is not what God is communicating to us, because He also gives us other commands about wisdom. He gives us instructions about not causing others to sin, and not enabling others to sin (1 Timothy 5:22).

Jesus Himself practiced godly boundaries, which we can see in action many times throughout the gospels. The people of Nazareth tried to kill Him. He left there and never returned. King Herod questioned Jesus, but Jesus refused to answer him. Jesus also routinely stood up to the religious leaders of His day, and he avoided the Jewish authorities many times when they were trying to seize him, arrest him, or kill him (see John 7:30-32, and John 10:31, 39).

A religious legalist might really struggle with the idea that Jesus was not "submitting to the earthly authorities" except for this one thing: They have no agenda which makes them want to interpret the Scripture that way. Religious legalists usually misapply Scripture in a way that serves their own agenda, or the agenda of the enemy. The enemy would love nothing more than for an abused woman to stay trapped in abuse until it ultimately takes her life. He seeks to steal, kill, and destroy.

If an abusive husband is truly repentant and in godly sorrow over his sin of abuse, his actions will prove that out. He will be willing to get help while giving his wife all the time and space she needs to be protected and safe while she heals. He will be willing to "gouge out his own eye" in order to stop sinning, meaning that he will be willing to go to any means necessary in order to make sure this sin never happens again.

A few tears shed at the altar is not enough. True repentance requires action. A woman is not required by the Bible to go back into a dangerous situation just because her husband verbally indicates repentance or shows some emotion. She can forgive and heal while also maintaining Christlike boundaries. Remember, Jesus got out of Nazareth when His physical safety was threatened!

What is the Right Approach?

So what can we do when we suspect abuse or we see it? First, let's talk about women who are not ready to fully admit to what's happening, or not ready to leave their abuser. Think back to all the reasons that we talked about for why an abused woman doesn't just leave. Knowing that, a more practical approach might be to start by asking the woman, "What can I do to help you?"

Ask what her tangible needs are. Ask what is something that is important to her that would help her feel empowered or back in control?

Her answer might be doing something as simple as running an errand for her. Taking her animal to the vet. It might seem trivial to you, but it's something that is important to her that she cannot do on her own. The important thing is, you'll be taking steps toward establishing trust with her, breaking the hold her abuser has over her, and helping her feel like she has some control.

This is all about helping the victim. We have to remember that she leads a lonely life. Try to be a friend to her. Pray with her. Ultimately, the goal is to help expose the secrecy and lies surrounding the situation.

If the woman or her children are in imminent danger, you can try to stage an intervention. When possible, it's best to contact professionals or volunteers who work in the area of domestic violence to help plan and execute such an intervention. You also want to notify law enforcement and see what they can do to help.

If the woman is already looking to get out of the situation, it's best to get a domestic violence organization or a battered women shelter involved. There is a national domestic hotline that anyone can call at any time. The number is 1-800-799-SAFE (7233).

Do whatever you can to get the victims to safety, but

don't stop there. Stay involved and keep following up with them. Stay as close as you can to the victim during this time, as it is crucial to her safety and well-being. As one of my mentors Debbie Stafford says, "The biggest concern in family violence situations is safety for the victims. Not only does a person deserve to *be* safe, they also deserve to *feel* safe." If she has to go to court, for example, her support team can go with her. Both the victim and the abuser need to see that the victim has a team of people standing at her side who are not going to tolerate any form of threats, abuse, or violence.

Combating the Lies: Lie #4 — You Are Trapped in Your Situation

Often, we believe the notion that there is no way out of an abusive situation. That is a lie.

> The weapons we fight with are not the weapons of the world. On the contrary, they have divine power to demolish strongholds.
>
> 2 Corinthians 10:4 NIV

Did you know there is a court in Heaven? The heavenly court is described in Daniel 7:9-10 and Psalm 82:1.

Did you know that the Bible calls Satan "the accuser of the brethren"? That means he is constantly hurling lies, slanders, and accusations at God's children. But we have an advocate in the heavenly court—Jesus, our mediator.

The enemy's harassment, intimidation, slander, and accusation are all designed to keep us trapped. However, the enemy does not have real power. Jesus has real power. The enemy's "power" is all based on lies. If he can get humans to believe his lies, he can keep them trapped. But when we replace the lies with God's truth, we are set free. Are you ready to be free? Pray this prayer:

Heavenly Father, I come into Your court covered by the blood of Jesus Christ. I know that it is not Your will for me to be abused physically, sexually, or mentally, or to be harmed in any manner. I ask You in the name of Jesus to issue a divine restraining order against my abusive partner. I enter Your courtroom with confidence and come boldly to the throne of grace because of the blood of Jesus. I am asking that any legal rights that the enemy had through generational sin or through my own actions be broken and abolished by the blood of Jesus. I ask that in Jesus' name any demonic powers behind the abuse will be restrained and void of power and control. I declare that the cycle of abuse and violence is broken. I ask You in the name of Jesus that a restraining order will be activated. I ask You as the righteous judge to assign angels on my behalf to carry out enforcement of this order on earth in my situation, for you have all authority. I also pray for the abuser's salvation and for You to bring him into healing and restoration. I thank You for Your protection and ask You to be Lord over any further interaction with _____ (the hurtful partner). In Jesus' name I pray, amen.

Getting and Staying Safe

When you have experienced an abusive relationship—whether you are still in that relationship or even if you consider it to be over—it's very important for you to have a network and to stay in frequent contact with your network. Here are some steps you can take to get started:

1. Tell someone about your situation. It can be someone at church, someone who works to help abused women, or someone in a support group.
2. Have a safety plan. Ideally, your plan will be developed in conjunction with an organization that helps abused women. It will normally involve having emergency contacts and having a bag packed that includes important documents and essentials. Even if you are already living on your own away from your abuser, you need to have a safe place where you and your children can take refuge should the abuser try to find you or contact you.
3. Pray. Ask for the Lord's protection and wisdom on how to proceed. Pray for Him to open a door and make the right path for you to get free of this situation permanently.
4. Be courageous. You must be strong and brave, especially if there are children involved. You must prioritize their safety, and you need to get authorities involved.
5. If you are currently in an unsafe situation such as living with your abuser or staying at a place where he has access to you, you must leave. Make sure you do it in a way that is safe. It's not wise to confront an abuser and tell them you're leaving, unless you have the authorities with you.
6. Stay safe! Often in the cycle of domestic violence,

we create boundaries and then we either violate them ourselves, or we allow our abuser to worm their way back in. Yes, you have invested emotions in the relationship. A big piece of you feels attached, but you cannot be driven by emotion on this. You must prioritize safety—physical, emotional, and spiritual.

Not being driven by emotions is, of course, easier said than done most of the time. Some tools are helpful in this regard. One tool I have used often throughout the years came from the book, *Codependency*, by Pat Springle. The tool could be called IDD, which stands for **Identify, Detach, Decide.**

When our emotions are wrapped up in a situation, we need to identify the behaviors, feelings, thoughts, and words that define our codependency. Once we recognize unhealthy behaviors, we can detach and reflect on the situation. We can think about new possible responses, rather than doing what we normally do. We can think through various ways of responding that are more healthy. After thinking through various possibilities, we can now decide what to do. Chances are, after going through that little exercise of **Identify**, **Detach**, and **Decide**, we are going to make a much healthier decision. We are much less likely to be driven along by our emotions.

Developing a Safety Plan

Safety plans are often specific to a person's situation and location. However, here are some good general principles to keep in mind for developing your safety plan:

1. Always keep some money hidden.
2. Make extra keys for the car and house.
3. Try to gather and keep important documents offsite, maybe at a trusted friend's house: Bank account information, insurance policies (or at least the contact person's #), marriage license, driver's license, social security numbers (both his and yours), birth certificates (your own and those of your children), and also vaccination records of children.
4. Make sure you have access to life-saving medications or have a plan to get them quickly.
5. Have a bag with all of your survival items well hidden somewhere nearby that he can't find it. Maybe a neighbor or trusted friend's house.
6. Know what his pattern of behavior is during the violent stage and determine where the best place would be to have these things readily available in case you need to leave quickly.
7. If possible, notify a neighbor to be alert to strange noises and call police for you.
8. Get rid of weapons in the house.
9. Do not use any social media.
10. Call police if needed!

Discussion Questions

1. Does any type of abuse discussed in this chapter apply to your current situation? Past situations?
2. If you are currently in an abusive situation, where are you at this moment in the cycle of abuse?
3. The victim is often made to feel like she needs to justify her own actions or choices. Which of your choices has your abuser made you defend to him?

FIVE

The Tie That Binds

Blessed be the tie that binds our hearts in Christian love. The fellowship of kindred minds is like to that above.

Composer John Fawcett

WE ARE all familiar with the good ties, such as family ties, the emotional bond between parent and child, or even among groups that share an ethnic or national identity. But there is also such a thing as ties which are not good or healthy. Most of us do not even think about these until presented with teachings from the Bible about what has come to be called "soul ties."

The Bible tells us that we are made in the image of God, "So God created human beings in his own image. In the image of God he created them; male and female he created them (Genesis 1:27 NLT). Just like God is a triune being made up of the Father, the Son (who came to earth in a physical body), and the Holy Spirit, we are also triune beings. We are made up of body, soul, and spirit, according to the Bible. "May God himself, the God of peace, sanctify you through and through. May your whole spirit, soul and body be kept blameless at the coming of our Lord Jesus Christ" (1 Thessalonians 5:23 NLT).

We are spirit beings who currently live in a physical body. The physical body also currently houses our soul, which is defined as our mind, will, and emotions. In Genesis chapter 2, we see a deep physical and emotional connection between the first-ever husband and wife.

> The man said, "This is now bone of my bones and flesh of my flesh; she shall be called 'woman,' for she was taken out of man. That is why a man leaves his father and mother and is united to his wife, and they become one flesh."
>
> Genesis 2:23-24 NIV

The two become one flesh. How do they do that? Through the sexual union. If you think about the physical act of sex, it very much fits that divine description. So God always intended for there to be a deep union which occurs and is expressed through the act of sex. This understanding of the passage in Genesis is further confirmed by the Holy Spirit writing through Paul to the Corinthians:

> Do you not know that your bodies are members of Christ himself? Shall I then take the members of Christ and unite them with a prostitute? Never! Do you not know that he who unites himself with a prostitute is one with her in

body? For it is said, "The two will become one flesh." But whoever is united with the Lord is one with him in spirit.

1 Corinthians 6:15-17 NIV

The Bible is clear. The act of sex results in a union of two people—a union that has consequences. Paul goes on to exhort the Corinthians:

Flee from sexual immorality. All other sins a person commits are outside the body, but whoever sins sexually, sins against their own body. Do you not know that your bodies are temples of the Holy Spirit, who is in you, whom you have received from God? You are not your own; you were bought at a price. Therefore honor God with your bodies.

1 Corinthians 6:18-20 NIV

Sexual immorality, meaning sex outside of marriage, affects our soul; our inner being. It has serious consequences, much more so than for many other types of sins. God always intended for the sexual union to be a bonding agent between husband and wife. He made it pleasurable and fun, yes, but only within the confines of healthy boundaries. Outside of the bonds of marriage, it leads to trouble and damage.

One of the major ways it causes damage is by forming what's known as a "soul tie." Simply put, a soul tie is a spiritual, physical, and emotional attachment to another person, usually formed through sexual activity. God intended this soul tie to be good and healthy. It's supposed to unite a husband and wife, making them inseparable. That's what God has always intended for marriage, as explained by Jesus in the book of Matthew, when he was asked about divorce:

> "Haven't you read," he replied, "that at the beginning the Creator 'made them male and female,' and said, 'For this reason a man will leave his father and mother and be united to his wife, and the two will become one flesh'? So they are no longer two, but one flesh. Therefore what God has joined together, let no one separate."
>
> Matthew 19:4-6 NIV

The sexual union is designed by God to help form a bond so strong that we become inseparable. Husbands and wives enter into what is intended to be a lifelong covenant relationship between themselves and God, and the plan is for them to remain with each other through any difficulties they might face. The sexual union is designed by God to help us walk out that plan for marriage. Imagine the problem created when we enter into that type of union with someone that we have not committed to be with for life.

Think of a soul tie as being like two pieces of paper glued together. If you try to take them apart, what happens? You will probably get a mess. They were entwined and meshed together. The papers have become attached to each other, and you can separate them, but they will no longer be whole and complete. They will be tattered, torn, and fragmented.

Another good illustration would be drinking way too

much alcohol at a party. You know that it might make you sick. It will definitely make you feel terrible the next day. You might act foolish or get into trouble. But for some reason, you do it anyway. After enough time, you build up a tolerance for the alcohol. It no longer makes you sick, and if you drink often enough and long enough, you will actually start to feel sick without it.

Toxic relationships turn into addictions. Just as with other addictions, you know it is not good for you, but you will run after it anyway. You start to think you can't live without it. Just like an alcoholic has sober moments when he wants to get away from the life he has created, you have moments of clarity when you realize it's not healthy and you want to get away. But you can't seem to break free. There is an unhealthy bond—a binding that has taken place—and it must be broken.

This is a perfect example of why God's boundaries are good and loving. When we're young, we often tend to think of God as the great party-pooper in the sky. He's just out to spoil our fun, telling us not to do all the things that we think are pleasurable. However, by the time our behavior runs its full course, we begin to recognize that He was right all along. His boundaries are for our own good, and He gives them to us out of His love for us, just as any good parent does with their children.

Some more illustrations using nature would be fires and rivers. A campfire is nice and useful. You can enjoy the warmth, roast hot dogs, and make smores. But outside of the confines of the fire pit, the fire can ravage beautiful landscapes, leaving destruction everywhere it touches. It's the same for a river. They are useful for so many things:

recreation, transport, water supplies, wildlife, and fishing. But once the boundaries are breached and a flood comes, there is terrible damage and destruction.

Sex is a gift from God. It's healthy and good within the confines of marriage, and He intended it for our enjoyment. But all kinds of problems develop when we engage in sex outside of God's boundaries. The visible ones are crisis pregnancies, disease, the breaking up of marriages, or psychological and emotional damage. But whenever people sin, they also open themselves up to unseen spiritual forces.

In my case, I believe that one of the factors which led me to abort without really questioning the decision was a soul tie that came through Louis. When Louis was younger, he had belonged to a street gang. One night, they were in a fight with a rival gang. After a chase, Louis and some others managed to catch one of the rival gang members. That led to the rival gang member being killed.

Louis was not the one who physically killed the rival gang member, but he was involved in capturing and trapping him. He was certainly an accessory to the man's murder, even though that was apparently not what he had in mind when he gave chase. Louis carried tremendous guilt over this, and I believe there was a spirit of murder which had attached itself to Louis.

As a result of my soul tie with Louis, I believe I had opened myself up to the influence of a spirit of murder.

More on Soul Ties

The term "soul tie" is not found in the Bible, but neither are the terms 'trinity,' 'rapture,' or "Great Commission."

However, those things are clearly described in the Bible, so the Church and theologians have assigned terms to them for ease of reference. It's the same with "soul tie." You may not hear them discussed very much on Sunday mornings, because the concept can come across as a bit spooky. However, spiritual forces are real, and Jesus never backed down from discussing the realities of Hell, the devil, or demons.

RC Blakes is a minister who often teaches on soul ties. At present, you can find his teachings on YouTube. In one of his video teachings,[1] he explains:

> The word soul-tie is formed from the two words: soul and tie. The soul (our mind, will, and emotions) and tie (the definition of which is to bind or lock down). So, our mind is bound. The ties wrap around the mind and create a longing. Have you ever wondered why you cannot stop thinking about a person? Invisible ties or chains are drawing you. Have you ever been with one person but thinking about someone else on the other side of town . . . The longer you are engaged in a soul tie relationship, the less capable you are of appreciating or recognizing real love the way God said a man should love a woman. Be careful to what low you allow yourself to sink. You may get stuck there. If you spend another five years in that relationship, you have wasted half a decade. How many times must he strike you before you realize that you should not be treated like this?
>
> Pastor RC Blakes, Jr

Having sexual relations with anyone other than your spouse is an act of him sinning against you, you sinning against him, and both of you sinning against God. This creates a soul tie.

It might be easier for women to become attached via a soul tie because we are generally more driven by emotion. Also, if you struggle with self-esteem, you can become easy prey as you look to another person as a source of your own self-worth.

The picture of sexual union again gives us a clue as to what goes on spiritually and emotionally. The man puts a "deposit" into the woman, even if she does not conceive. Part of him is left inside of her.

The Root of the Problem

It often surprises people to find out that the root of sexual sin is not sex. Sex is good. This is the clear teaching of the Bible. God also tells us that the original root of sexual sin is actually pride. It's pride that causes us to reject God, and when we reject God as our God—our loving Father, Ruler, and King—we are left to pursue "dishonorable passions." The first chapter of Romans explains the problem this way:

> For although they knew God, they neither glorified him as God nor gave thanks to him, but their thinking became futile and their foolish hearts were darkened . . . Therefore God gave them over in the sinful desires of their hearts to sexual impurity for the degrading of their bodies with one another. They exchanged the truth about God for a lie, and worshiped and served created things rather than the

Creator . . . Because of this, God gave them over to shameful lusts. Even their women exchanged natural sexual relations for unnatural ones.

Romans 1:21, 24-26 NIV

The nature of pride is to be completely self-centered and consume. Pride sees God's creation, including other people, as objects to be used for feeding one's own selfish desires. This is true of sexual sin just like it is greed, drunkenness, or gluttony. Selfish desire is the birthplace of addiction, or bondage.

Freedom is found in the belief that we are not our own. We were created by someone else, and we answer to Him. God paid a very dear price for us when He sent His Son, Jesus, to die on a cross so that we could be redeemed. Understanding that we are His is actually what liberates us to be what He created us to be.

The Role of Abuse

The word 'abuse' comes from putting together two other words: 'abnormal' and 'use.' You will not be able to use anything in the right way until you know how it was designed to be used. God's design for His creation is perfect and authoritative, so if you use anything for a purpose other than what He intended, the result is "abnormal use"—that is, abuse!

If a man does not know or understand the purpose of a wife, he will end up using her in ways other than what God intended. He will abuse her.

The same can be true of men who were not our husbands. For example, women can be forced into submissive roles by controlling leaders such as parents, teachers, boyfriends, pimps, drug dealers, cult leaders, and so on. Sometimes even pastors or other church leaders abuse people under their care. Sexual bonding is the most common form of an unholy soul tie, but it can also happen through other types of abuse, control, manipulation, or other inappropriate behavior. When these things take place, an unholy soul tie is formed.

If you have experienced something like this, it is not your fault! You are not the one who is morally responsible for what happened to you. And God will deal with the injustice.

Other Types of Soul Ties

Soul ties can also be formed with places and institutions. For example, maybe you get a sick feeling when you drive by an abortion clinic. Others might have fear and anxiety when driving past an old house or neighborhood where they were abused. Another common example might be feelings of guilt and torment when passing a hotel where an affair took place. We can develop unholy soul ties through associations with sinful party lifestyles, drug culture, music culture, or occult practices, and we might experience emotional turmoil when coming into contact with those things even years down the road.

Soul ties that are developed through our own sinful behavior often strengthen over time. For example, the more a person uses drugs, the more they will be "bound" by that sin. When our own sin is involved, the soul tie really is a lordship issue. "Thou shalt have no other gods before me." If we choose not to detach from any soul tie—even one that we did not cause—we are choosing the soul tie over God. That means it is a form of idolatry.

We can be saved, but still carrying many soul ties. Often, people receive Christ as Savior, but still need to go through a process of getting free from these types of attachments. The good news is, we can get free, and we'll go over how to do that at the end of the chapter. But first, there's one more type of soul tie we need to examine.

The Nature of Trauma

There are many Bible characters who faced significant trauma in their lives. Perhaps the most notable is Job. In chapter one of Job, we see that he was a blameless and upright man who feared God. He had so much wealth that he was considered to be the greatest of all men in the East. Job was going through his daily life when one day, a servant came to tell him that an enemy attacked, killed all of his other servants, and took all of his oxen and donkeys.

Before that lone survivor was done telling the story, one of Job's shepherds arrived. He reported that fire fell from the sky, burning up all of Job's sheep and the rest of the shepherds. This shepherd was the only one who escaped alive.

Yet again, another servant arrived on the scene, this one from the group that took care of Job's camels. He reported that raiders came and killed all of the other camel herders and stole all of Job's camels.

He is still telling the story, when finally a servant comes

on the scene to report that a whirlwind had come and destroyed the house where all ten of Job's children were gathered. They all died instantly. The servant was the only survivor who escaped to tell the story.

The trauma Job experienced was beyond comprehension.

As if all this weren't enough, we find that later on, Job is struck with painful sores from the crown of his head to the soles of his feet. Three of Job's friends came to be with him. His suffering was so great that they just sat on the ground with him for seven days and seven nights without saying a word.

The text does not tell us this, but I have to wonder whether the condition of Job's soul—agony, torment, and grief—somehow enabled the physical pain he endured in chapter two. The Bible does indicate in various places that there is a connection between the state of our souls and the health of our bodies. For example, we read in 3 John 1:2 (NKJV), "Beloved, I pray that you may prosper in all things and be in health, just as your soul prospers."

Many times, our outward pain is a reflection of our inner pain. In the fifth chapter of Mark, we find the story of a woman who had chronic bleeding from her uterus. The bleeding had lasted for twelve years. She had gone to many doctors and they only left her worse off, both physically and financially. On top of that, the woman was in deep humiliation and rejection because her bleeding meant that she was unclean under Mosaic law.

She could not have direct physical contact with anyone else. So imagine that when she walks down the street, people move away from her. No hugs. No kisses. Total physical isolation for twelve years. Most of the time, she probably did not go out of her house. And when she did, she had to be very careful not to even get close to others so as to avoid touching them accidentally.

We see this in the account in Mark. The woman knew that it would be improper for her to touch Jesus, but in faith, she thought to herself, "If I can simply touch the edge of His garment, I will be healed." Can you imagine the trauma involved in having no human contact for twelve years?

In 2 Corinthians 11:23-25, Paul recounts his personal sufferings and trauma. He had been imprisoned, beaten with rods, had received thirty-nine lashes on three different occasions, had been stoned, and had suffered through shipwrecks three different times. Jesus Himself experienced unbearable emotional pain in the Garden of Gethsemane, and equally terrible physical pain on the cross. The Bible doesn't simply acknowledge human suffering, it is actually one of the central themes.

Trauma wounds our souls. When people sin against us, it wounds our inner person. Not everyone has experienced the pain of abuse or the trauma of abortion. But most people have experienced mental and emotional wounds in their lives, whether it be from family issues, divorce, bankruptcy, job loss, injuries, or illnesses. Whatever the source, the pain is real and a wounded soul affects our thinking. Our ability to make good decisions is often hindered by the damage life inflicts on us.

This effect is magnified during pregnancy, when many chemical changes are occurring. So when a woman has experienced trauma, is currently under a lot of stress, and is also undergoing major changes to brain and body chemistry, the last thing she needs is to make a decision under pressure. Major life decisions should never be rushed.

Trauma has a major, lasting effect on individuals. As Dr. Phil often says, "Trauma changes who we are." If we take some time to reflect on that statement, most of us will find it to be true in our own lives. We're different than we were before the trauma.

Dr. Vincent Rue is a psychotherapist, researcher, consultant, and founder of the Director of the Institute for Pregnancy Loss, an independent non-profit research and treatment center. Dr. Rue has a PhD in Child Development and Family Relations. In 1981, Dr. Rue provided the first clinical evidence of postabortion trauma, identifying this psychological condition as "Postabortion Syndrome" in testimony before the U.S. Congress. Over the years he has treated numerous men and women who have been traumatized by their abortion experience. He is well known and respected in the pro-life community.

It occurred to me that I had read or heard somewhere that abortion was listed as a reason for PTSD in the Diagnostic and Statistical Manual of Mental Disorder, which is used by health care professionals as a guide to the diagnosis of mental disorder.

I contacted Dr. Rue with my question and his response astounded me. He told me the American Psychiatric Association had purged abortion from DSM IV and V. It was last seen in the DSM III. I asked if he knew the reason, and his response is as follows:

"I suspect there may be two reasons why the American Psychiatric Association deleted 'abortion' as a type of psychosocial stressor capable of causing Posttraumatic Stress

Disorder (PTSD) from its *Diagnostic & Statistical Manual of Mental Disorders – Fourth Edition* (DSM-IV)

1. Anne Speckhard and I published the first peer-reviewed and invited article on post-abortion syndrome in the Journal of Social Issues (i) (a premier professional journal of the American Psychological Association) in 1992.

2. After publication of this article, I received a cease and desist letter from the general counsel of the American Psychiatric Association threatening me that if I persisted in identifying the aftereffects of abortion as a type of PTSD, that they would take legal action against me. I wrote back that as a licensed mental health professional, my diagnosis was accurate for the patients I treated and I would not cease writing and lecturing on the topic, to which they never responded. Instead, I suspect their response a year and a half later was to simply remove the word "abortion" from the updated version of the DSM III-R, the SCM-IV, so as to not provide any possible professional/clinical support that abortion could cause psychological injury."

Dr. Vincent Rue

There you have it. I would simply add that if no women experience some form of trauma or PTSD after abortion, why are groups such as the Silent No More Awareness Campaign growing in numbers? And why are so many abortion recovery groups out there? Why would they be necessary if abortion were not traumatic for so many women?

Traumatic Bonding Through Abuse

Traumatic bonding is defined as the strong emotional ties that develop between two persons where one person intermittently harasses, beats, threatens, abuses, or intimidates the other (Dutton and Painter, 1981).[2] One person will dominate the other and the abuse levels rise and fall. This process becomes emotionally difficult due to not knowing what to expect. The behavior goes from affectionate to abusive and back again. It is a destructive and powerful bond, sporadic in nature, and it thrives in relationship with a deep imbalance of power.

Traumatic bonding differs from a healthy bonding process because healthy bonding is affectionate and protective. Traumatic bonding is not protective and is instead based on jealousy, manipulation, and control. As previously noted, the imbalance of power is often maintained by isolation and threats, especially if the woman doesn't freely submit to the control.

Whenever pain is inflicted by one of the parties in a relationship, some form of traumatic bonding occurs. The more traumatic the bond, the harder it is for a woman to leave. If we think of common soul ties as being two pieces of paper held together by glue, we can think of deep trauma and abuse as being like two pieces of cardboard held together by super glue.

Just as a woman becomes bonded or addicted to any toxic or dysfunctional relationship, the battered, deeply traumatized woman becomes bonded to her abuser, even though she lives in constant fear of him. She becomes hooked on the intermittence of the relationship because she still craves affection, and receives it during the honeymoon phase. Her need for affection is likely increased due to the battery and abuse, further exacerbating her dependence on the abuser. In an effort to survive, and possibly also to hide their shame, the victim will often deny the reality of the abuse both to themselves and others.

When people outside of the relationship do see signs of abuse, or see it firsthand, they often get tired of seeing it or hearing about it. The reason is that they try to help, but it does not seem to do any good. It's painful to watch, so they ultimately check out of the situation emotionally. After enough time and effort with no good result, they might start to see the situation as essentially hopeless. This is similar to a cycle that family and friends experience when a loved one is living with severe drug or alcohol addiction. As a result, the victim of abuse begins to see themselves as weak, and they fear criticism from anyone who learns of the abuse.

Breaking Soul Ties

If you recognize any of these things in yourself, the good news is that soul ties can be broken! In fact, some soul ties can be broken quite easily. Others can take a little more work, especially if they have become deeply entrenched.

Step 1: Right now, take a moment to ask the Lord to bring to your mind any trauma or wounding in your life. Ask Him to show you any unhealthy ties you have in your life.

This step is crucial because we are often holding on to things in our lives that we aren't even aware of—things which can give the enemy a foothold in our lives. We have authority over the enemy, but we sometimes yield that authority to him. We are usually unaware that we are doing this. The Holy Spirit gladly answers this prayer. He is ready and willing to work in you and heal you. As He brings things to your mind, write them down. Make a list.

Step 2: Confess your sins to God, and turn away from them. Repent for whatever part you had in becoming involved in a particular situation, or for staying in it. For abuse in which you were the victim and had no moral responsibility (such as abuse that happened when you were a child), then this step doesn't apply to those particular instances. But you can go ahead and ask God to deliver you, heal you, and enable you to walk in freedom. Part of this process is forgiving the person or people who abused you.

Forgiveness does not mean that the person who abused you was right. Your forgiveness of a person is not the same thing as condoning their behavior. You are not even excusing their behavior. Healthy boundaries are Christlike and biblical, so forgiveness does not mean that you must let a person back into your life. Rather, forgiveness simply means that we do not hold a person liable in our own hearts. Instead, we turn the person and the situation completely over to God. Picture yourself with invisible chains wrapped around you and bound tightly with locks. When you forgive a person, you are simply unlocking those chains, setting them on the ground, and walking away free.

Forgiveness also is not a feeling. Sometimes people get the impression that they must "feel" like they have forgiven a person before they can forgive. That is not true. Forgiveness is a choice we make. The feelings of freedom follow our decision to forgive, not the other way around. Going back to our metaphor, you won't "feel" that the chains are off until you make the decision to unlock them and set them on the ground. Here's the reality that is sometimes hard for us to accept: God forgives us, and He requires us to forgive others.

> And whenever you stand praying, if you have anything against anyone, forgive him, that your Father in heaven may also forgive you your trespasses. But if you do not forgive, neither will your Father in heaven forgive your trespasses.
>
> Mark 11:25-26 NKJV

We all have a debt of sin that we would never be able to repay. I don't want to pay for my own sin by being cast into Hell for all of eternity. Do you? I hope that you don't. But receiving God's forgiveness clearly means forgiving others. So let's do that now. You can make a choice to forgive in this moment. Here is a prayer you can pray right now to forgive those who have wronged you, and to break off any and every ungodly attachment in your life:

> *Father, in the name of Jesus, I submit my soul, my desires, and my emotions to Your Spirit. I repent for any part I played in my trauma, for any part of the trauma that was my fault, or for any pain I have afflicted upon anyone. I repent of all anger, bitterness, resentment, and wrong attitudes toward those who have hurt me. I choose with Your help to forgive anyone and*

everyone associated with the trauma—every family member, spouse, partner, friend, or co-worker.

I make a choice today to forgive my abuser—and indeed everyone who has ever hurt or abused me in any way—just as You have forgiven me.

I confess as sin all of my promiscuous, premarital sexual relationships and all sexual relationships outside of marriage, along with all emotional affairs that caused a soul tie. I confess all of my ungodly and unholy soul ties of spirit, soul, and body as sin.

I ask you to loose me from all soul ties to my past sexual partners and ungodly relationships. I forgive anyone who has manipulated or molested me, or anyone who played a part in any sexual abuse. I ask you to release me by the holy blood of Jesus Christ from any torment in my mind, soul, or body. I need the blood of Jesus and I thank You for the blood of Jesus. I declare in faith that His blood has the power to heal any wound or trauma at its source, at the point of entry where it came into my life. Whether it was caused by generational sins or curses, word curses, or sin committed by me or against me, the blood of Jesus washes me clean and makes me whole.

I thank You that the blood You shed on the cross flows to the source of my wound. I thank You that it removes any trauma, hurt, pain, sickness, confusion, and anything that is not from You—anything You did not create to be a part of me in Your perfect design for me. I thank You, Lord, that I am free of depression, guilt, agony, shame, and anger. I thank You that I am of sound mind, free of any emotional sickness, and am healed in body and soul.

And I thank You that my body will no longer hold the memory of trauma that I have endured. I thank You that I am totally free, and I claim supernatural and accelerated recovery from all hurt and trauma in Jesus' name. Amen.

Step 3: Take communion. It heals the soul and body. You do not need to be in a church service to partake of communion. Communion is between you and the Lord. Communion is not an institution of the church. It is a personal thing; it is an act of drawing near and creating a fellowship with Him. Thank Him for the bread, which provides strength and represents His body. His body was broken for you and by His wounds, you are healed. Jesus is the bread of life!

The juice or wine represents His blood that was shed for you and cleanses all sin. It purifies and washes you clean. This pertains to all sin.

Step 4: Fill up the empty space with the Holy Spirit. Anytime we get delivered from things that were taking place in our lives, we need to fill that empty space with the things of God.

> "When an evil spirit leaves a person, it goes into the desert, seeking rest but finding none. Then it says, 'I will return to the person I came from.' So it returns and finds its former home empty, swept, and in order. Then the spirit finds seven other spirits more evil than itself, and they all enter the person and live there. And so that person is worse off than before.
>
> Matthew 12:43-45 NLT

Filling yourself up with the things of God takes work, but trust me, it's a lot easier and more beneficial than being held captive by the devil. So make sure you have a daily routine of prayer, Bible study, and close fellowship with the Lord. I also recommend creating a small list of Bible verses that you read and declare over your life daily. Here is a small list to help you get started.

> Therefore, if anyone is in Christ, the new creation has come: The old has gone, the new is here!
>
> 2 Corinthians 5:17 NIV

> Therefore, I urge you, brothers and sisters, in view of God's mercy, to offer your bodies as a living sacrifice, holy and pleasing to God—this is your true and proper worship. Do not conform to the pattern of this world, but be transformed by the renewing of your mind. Then you will be able to test and approve what God's will is—his good, pleasing and perfect will.
>
> Romans 12:1-2 NIV

> For the Spirit God gave us does not make us timid, but gives us power, love and self-discipline.
>
> 2 Timothy 1:7 NIV

> He sent His word and healed them,
>   And delivered them from their destructions.

> Psalm 107:20 NKJV

> He restores my soul;
>> He leads me in the paths of righteousness
>> For His name's sake.
>
> Psalm 23:3 NKJV

> Brothers and sisters, I do not consider myself yet to have taken hold of it. But one thing I do: Forgetting what is behind and straining toward what is ahead.
>
> Philippians 3:13 NIV

Continue to turn away from your sins, your unhealthy emotional bonds, and the effects of trauma. Keep taking communion. Keep praying. Keep claiming God's promises, and declaring scripture over your life. As you do these things, your healing will become more and more complete. God does perform miraculous, instantaneous healing of the soul sometimes just like He does with the body. But for most of us, it is a process that will take some time and effort.

Don't be discouraged. The Lord is faithful. If you had a deadly disease, and God told you He was going to heal you through diet, exercise, and medicine, you would undoubtedly keep doing all of those things. He is going to heal your soul. Keep repeating these steps as often as you need to, and don't give up. God loves you. He is for you. And He wants His best for you.

The more you repeat the process, the more you are being

built up to be stronger, more resilient, and healthier than ever before. Did you know that if you cut a board and then use wood glue to bind it back together, it will be stronger than it was before? It's the same with this process.

Another illustration is to think of an old house that is being remodeled. The first thing you have to do is tear out the old material to make room for the new. Items get moved around. Dust and debris get everywhere. Rooms become disorganized and crowded. It can be a messy and frustrating time, but well worth it when you get to see and enjoy the finished product.

You're not just under construction, you're being renovated and reconstructed with better and stronger materials. Yes, trauma changes who we are. But when we get on the other side of God's healing process, we are transformed into His likeness. He can actually make us more whole than we were before the trauma.

Trust that through this process, He is making you whole and complete in Him.

Combating the Lies: Lie #5—You are Damaged Beyond Repair

When we have committed abortion, there is trauma. When we have suffered abuse, there is pain and damage in our hearts and minds. Our souls carry the emotional scars of the past. However, we do not have to live in that hurt. We can experience freedom. We can heal. And we can move forward, fully redeemed and restored.

> Then you will know the truth, and the truth will set you free.

Healing Hidden Bruises

John 8:32 NIV

So if the Son sets you free, you will be free indeed.

John 8:36 NIV

It is for freedom that Christ has set us free. Stand firm, then, and do not let yourselves be burdened again by a yoke of slavery.

Galatians 5:1 NIV

He personally carried our sins
>   in his body on the cross
> so that we can be dead to sin
>   and live for what is right.
> By his wounds
>   you are healed.

1 Peter 2:24 NLT

For I will restore health to you,
>   and your wounds I will heal,
> declares the Lord,
>   because they have called you an outcast:
>   'It is Zion, for whom no one cares!'

Jeremiah 30:17 NIV

He heals the brokenhearted

and binds up their wounds.

> Psalm 147:3 NIV

Do you still struggle with memories of your abortion? Do you still struggle with painful memories of the abuse? If so, I want you to picture one of those memories right now. The Lord can take you back to that memory. Only, this time, He will be there with you. When you picture that memory in your mind, say, "Lord, I need you to heal me of this memory. Would you please heal me of this memory?" And then wait a moment or two. Keep the memory in your mind, but also notice as He lifts the pain and trauma associated with that memory. All of a sudden, the thought will leave you and it generally will not come back. If it ever does come back briefly, it does not hurt the way it did before. It's only there as reference material. The memory no longer has a hold on you. God has sent out His Word to heal you, and He has delivered you from the destruction. You are healed in Jesus' name.

Now that you've experienced this simple healing process, you know what to do. Every time a painful memory of any kind comes to your mind, just repeat these simple steps with the Lord. Holy Spirit will be right there with you and He will place His healing balm on each and every wound. Typically, you will experience quite a few of these moments for the first several months. But as time wears on, you will have less and less wounds to heal, so it won't happen as often. Still, you can expect that the Lord may bring painful memories to your mind here and there over the next year or two—each time with the purpose of healing you. Just ask and He will do it.

Discussion Questions

1. Have you ever developed any non-sexual soul ties?
2. What kind of experience did you have praying through painful memories?
3. After going through this chapter, do you feel like you are still struggling with any soul ties?
4. Is anything else on your heart to share?

SIX

Understanding the Grieving Process

YEARS AGO, a mentor told me something that struck me as profound. She said, "The basis of any support group is that of unresolved grief."

Understanding unresolved grief is a major key to healing, but before we can thoroughly explore unresolved grief, it helps to have knowledge of the grief cycle. The first thing most of us probably do not realize about grief is that every change in life will initiate some level of grief—even the good changes, like marriage or a job promotion.

For example, a job promotion results in better pay, but it almost always means more responsibility, greater stress, and longer hours too. The established routine of life will be interrupted, and this will cause some level of grief. Marriage is wonderful and the wedding is an immensely joyful occasion. But soon after the wedding, newlyweds often find that their expectations are not being met. They find that it's harder than they imagined, and might even begin to feel like their notions about married life were highly idealistic.

Grief entered our world when the first human beings sinned, and it is an unavoidable part of life. Our grief is not always the direct result of someone's sin, but we do experience grief when someone violates God's laws—either ourselves or someone connected to us. In these cases, we may understand that something is wrong, but we may not recognize what we're going through as part of the grief cycle. Examples might be in cases of abuse. We know that something is wrong and that we're affected by what happened, but we may not understand what we're experiencing as being grief.

American culture has collectively decided to allow around three days off from work when a relative passes away. That barely gives us time to arrange and have a funeral. It doesn't give us any time or space to go through the grieving process, and it's almost absurd to think we can return to normal life after three days.

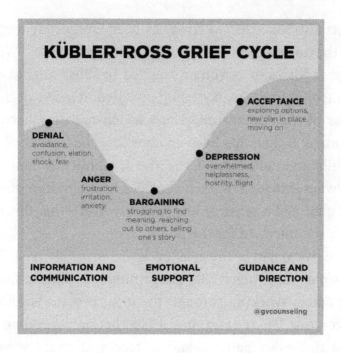

The preceding graphic[1] shows the grief cycle as originally described by Elisabeth Kubler-Ross in her 1969 book, *On Death and Dying*. Although the cycle was originally mapped out as a tool to help people who had terminal illnesses, the mental health profession has since widely adopted the cycle as a model for those mourning the loss of loved ones, as well as going through difficult events like divorce or job loss.

In the case of a woman caught in a cycle of violence, she has lost much of her own identity. She has lost the right to think and act for herself, and to be the free moral agent God intends her to be. She has probably lost the freedom to pursue her own dreams and goals. To some degree, she has lost the ability to come and go as she pleases. Social structure, family relationships, friendships, and other types of relational support are often missing from her life. Last, she has also lost trust, as trust has been completely removed from the one relationship which dominates her life.

Other losses by a woman trapped in abuse might be loss of control of finances, not being included in major decisions, or loss of her "dream" marriage which has now become a nightmare. If there has been an abortion, she faces the loss of her child and motherhood, the loss of identity as the mother she always intended to be. If she does have children, she may carry guilt and a sense of loss for their lives—that this is not the life she intended for them.

The five stages of the grief cycle are generally regarded as 1) Denial 2) Anger 3) Bargaining 4) Depression 5) Acceptance. Working through the grief process is different for everyone. There is no rule or law that says everyone must follow this exact pattern, and in fact, you might see some versions of the model that switch the order of the bargaining and depression stages. It's possible for a person to go through any of the stages in any order, and it's even possible for people to skip one or more phases entirely.

There is also no set amount of time in regard to how long it should take to work through the various stages or through the total cycle. One person might move quickly through one phase and very slowly through another. What the Kubler-Ross cycle does provide is a model to help us understand what people most commonly experience during times in their lives when they are grieving. The more we understand, the more likely we are to work through grief in healthy ways and to help others do the same, so we will need to dig a little deeper into the different stages. We will spend the majority of our discussion on the anger and bargaining phases, since those phases are the most complex in regard to identifying where we are in the grieving process.

The Shock and Denial Phase

Shock and anger can go together. If you think about a scenario in which a person hits another person unexpectedly, the victim's reaction might be shock, accompanied immediately by intense anger. However, when faced with the sudden, unexpected departure of a loved one, most people do not experience anger in the early phases of grief. Exceptions might be cases where the loved one has been the victim of violence. But for other types of deaths like accidents or unexpected medical events, most of us would find ourselves thinking, "This can't be happening. This isn't true."

It's helpful to understand that the denial stage is basically a survival tool, or a coping mechanism. It provides an emotional cushion, of sorts, to help us come to terms with the new reality we are facing. Without this tool of shock, a person might be more likely to do something drastic, like harming themselves or others, or even drifting into some type of mental breakdown.

In the case of abortion, it is sometimes easier to stay in the denial phase for very long periods than it is with other types of loss. One reason for that is that after an abortion, we might be taught that we are not supposed to grieve. On top of that, we are not given a body to bury. There are no tangible remnants of the life of the child, like clothing or other personal belongings. There were no precious memories made. What we do have is the void created by a life that was taken before entering into 'life' as we know it.

When someone has believed things like that abortion was the right decision, or that they only removed some clumps of cells from their body, they are effectively in the denial phase. They can even stay stuck there long periods of time, only to find out later on that they had been saddled by repressed grief and guilt for years. In the book, *Forbidden Grief*, the authors describe a lady named Caitlyn who had her "defense mechanisms firmly in place" for 6 years after her abortion. However, when she was told by the veterinarian that her new puppy had serious health problems and needed to be put to sleep, her defenses collapsed.

She told the veterinarian that she could not allow something to be killed like this, and in that moment, the memory of her abortion came rushing to the surface. She felt physically sick, and then had the thought, "Well, you killed your baby. Why can't you let your dog die?" Caitlyn then describes having what sounds like a panic attack, with her legs shaking and feeling unable to breathe.

Caitlyn's problems did not stop there, as she seemed unable to cope with the death of the dog after the procedure. She cried daily for almost a year, even at work or around other people, and all her friends thought she was ridiculous. What Caitlyn experienced was a powerful mental connector which brought out her feelings of guilt, remorse, and grief over the loss of her baby. However, without proper support and understanding, Caitlyn struggled to understand what was happening and process her grief in a healthy way.

Another powerful example of the denial phase occurred in Kathy Whaling, who has given us permission to share her story. Kathy had three daughters that lived through the Columbine shooting. Along with the entire community, Kathy's daughters struggled terribly with grief and anger over the death of their classmates.

Kathy also found herself dealing with intense anger—not so much directed at Dylan Klebold and Eric Harris, but rather at their parents. She blamed them for what happened.

With the help of Christian counseling, Kathy's daughters eventually began to heal, but she found that she could not. Finally, in desperation, she decided to try counseling for herself. The counselor advised Kathy to either write a letter to the boys' parents, and then not send it, or simply make the choice to forgive. Kathy prayed about it, saying basically, "Lord, why should I forgive them?"

In that moment, Kathy felt the Lord pointing out that He had already forgiven her for the same thing Dylan and Eric did. At that point, Kathy realized that her own long-buried secret could no longer remain in the dark. She had previously had two abortions. She had to come to terms with the fact that she had taken human lives and was no "better" than anyone else who had sinned. Kathy's story was also shared in more detail in the book, *Motherhood Interrupted*, which I recommend as a good resource.

Anger

At some point, usually when the initial shock and denial begins to wind down somewhat, we might find ourselves angry. We wonder how life can continue without the person who left us. We often wrestle deeply with questions of why. Why now? Why these circumstances? Why did this happen to such a good person? Why did this happen to someone that others were depending on?

During this phase, it is possible for people to become angry at God as they question why He did not prevent the death or the circumstances that caused it. A person can spend a good deal of time in the anger phase, and they might go back and forth between the anger and depression phases. Sometimes depression itself can lead to anger, as a person begins to feel more hurts or pains they were not previously aware of. Having anger does not necessarily mean a person is working through the stages of grief. It's important to find the root cause of the anger in order to work through it in a healthy way, using the anger as a grieving tool to help a person heal.

Anger can be a double-edged sword. It can be constructive or destructive. Examples of destructive anger are outbursts, rage, desires for revenge, or seeking to harm another person. Anger is sometimes used as a mask to keep from dealing with the real reason we are hurting. For some people, hurt and anger often go hand in hand.

Constructive anger is the result of being harmed by another person or entity, and it can be considered healthy in the sense that it lets us know something is wrong. It serves as a built-in barometer, alerting us that something in our lives has been violated, that a boundary has been broken. The key is to channel that anger into a constructive action, like setting up better protections. Seeking justice for victims of wrongdoing, or seeking to make positive changes, are also examples of using anger in a constructive way.

Candace Lightner, the lady who started MADD (Mothers Against Drunk Driving), lost her daughter when a drunk driver hit and killed her in 1980. She spent the next 5 years building MADD, raising awareness of the problem, and successfully lobbying to have stricter drunk driving laws enacted all over the United States. John Walsh, the TV personality who hosted *America's Most Wanted* for many years to help law enforcement track down fugitives, is another example. He began his work as a victim rights advocate and criminal investigator after losing his son in a homicide.

As the Apostle Paul writes in Ephesians, "Be angry..." In that part, he's letting us know that the constructive phase of anger is not only acceptable, but it is good. However, Paul acknowledges the destructive side of anger when he continues, "... yet do not sin."

Anger can be a very difficult emotion to handle. Frequently, when a new hurt or offense occurs, it is heaped on top of previous hurts or offenses which we have not properly healed from. As a result, we end up with a big pile of anger and hurt.

In fact, it might be helpful to think of the anger in your life as being like a big pile of rocks. It's not possible for you to remove them all at once. You have to deal with them one stone at a time. Once the pile begins to dwindle, it starts to become easier and easier to deal with any new offenses or hurts that arise, just like it would be a lot easier and less overwhelming to deal with a single stone, than a large pile.

As mentioned previously, anger can be turned into activism. However, anyone setting out on that path would be wise to have some close friends and counselors help them examine their motives and make sure they are doing this from a healthy place. For example, you might ask, "Is my fighting attitude coming from the fact that I am no longer able to fight for the life of my loved one?" If so, it might be helpful to work at processing the anger to make sure it is not only constructive to society, but constructive to your own soul.

Some very good and healthy ways to process anger are to go to professional counseling. Sharing your emotions with others in support groups is another great way. Writing out a letter to the person you're angry with—not to send but strictly as a therapeutic tool—is also a good step. And last, physical exercise actually helps many women cope better with anger.

Bargaining

In the bargaining stage, a person is looking for a way to regain control. Bargaining helps postpone some of the sadness we experience. Frequently, this is the stage where we wrestle with the "what if" and "if only" questions and statements. Frequently, a person will try to make a deal with God, promising to do certain things in exchange for relief or healing from the intense pain one is experiencing. Bargaining with God in this way should not be considered as correct or healthy from a Christian point of view, because the Bible teaches that we are His daughters, dearly loved, bought and paid for by the death of God's Son. We do not have to play "Let's Make a Deal" with Him.

Bargaining is effectively an effort to change the outcome of an event. Women in abusive situations may find themselves often in the bargaining phase. Sadly, we may think things like, "If I can be a better wife, and stop nagging, then he will not get angry anymore. If I can just avoid doing the things that trigger his anger, he won't treat me like that." These kinds of thoughts can sometimes continue even after the relationship ends, e.g., "He is really a good person, if only he hadn't been abused as a child." The "if only" types of thoughts can be particularly concerning for a woman who has only recently removed herself physically from an abusive situation. She may still be very emotionally attached to the relationship.

When that is the case, it is crucial for the woman to come to terms with the reality that all of her hope is false. It is in vain. We must give up the hope that the other person will change. This is essentially giving up what has developed into an idol in our lives. We do not need any other person to treat us a certain way or spend time with us, or be in a relationship with us, in order to find our self-worth. Again, this is a lordship issue. True hope, contentment, and fulfillment must be found in the Lord. He is the only one who can heal us and bring us peace.

Bargaining also plays a big part in the grief process for an abortion. When the emotional pain and guilt begin to set in, a woman might try to justify or rationalize her decision. She may tell herself things like, "I didn't want to do this, but it was my only choice," or "I know abortion is wrong, but I had to do it." In a sense, she is trying to cut the grieving process short.

I would note that those kinds of statements often correctly describe how a woman feels when she makes the choice to abort. Because women do very often feel that they don't want to abort, but that it is the only option, or that they are under coercion from others. Sadly, it reminds me of an animal that is caught in a trap and chews off its own leg to get free. The poor creature doesn't want to do this, but feels that this is the only way out. However, these kinds of statements are made to one's self in the hope of stopping the pain one feels. The unfortunate result of making these statements to ourselves is that the grief cycle is interrupted.

When a woman has stopped her own grieving process short, she may pick up later on down the road with the process, even though she doesn't realize that is what's happening. For example, a woman who has gone through abortion and later recognized it as wrong might start speaking out about abortion. She may join protests. However, if she hasn't completed her grief cycle and gone through a healing process, her true motivation might be that she is trying to atone for the abortion she had. That could be true, even though in her mind she is merely trying to make a difference, given women facts about abortion, etc.

Another common bargaining tool that occurs among women who have not completed the grieving process is that they become involved in childcare, or perhaps start teaching children's classes at church. There is nothing wrong with these activities, of course, but it's good for a woman to examine the motive behind her actions just to make sure she has properly grieved and healed. If you find yourself in that situation, just ask, Am I doing these things to try to appease a guilty conscience? Deep down, do I believe that I need to somehow atone for my abortion in order to erase my guilt?

Another common bargaining tool we observe in post-abortive women are attempts to become a super mom to her own children. She may try to lead every group that involves her kids, keep the house immaculate for them, or even become more devoted to a career in an attempt to provide every material thing her children might want. This type of bargaining is doomed to fail because none of us are superhuman. When a woman attempts to become a super mom and then fails, the result is often depression.

Sadly, one of the most common bargaining tools is to have another baby. Having another baby is perfectly good and healthy, unless the underlying motivation is to somehow compensate for or replace the lost child. This phenomenon is sometimes referred to as a "replacement baby" or an "atonement child." A woman may tell herself something like, "If I have another chance, I will do better this time. I will make the right choice." Frequently, the woman will desire the replacement baby to be fathered by the same man that fathered her aborted baby. In some cases, a woman may even convince herself that she can somehow produce a duplicate of the baby she aborted.

This is not a healthy perspective, and it is also not true. Every baby is designed by God to be unique. Aborted babies are in Heaven. Any new pregnancy is a different baby. It's best to go through the grieving and healing process first whenever possible. Sometimes women report that when they are giving birth, memories of their prior abortion come rushing in.

Biblically, the word "atonement" was used in the Old Testament primarily to refer to sacrifices that a priest would make on behalf of the people. The priest would offer animals as a sacrifice to cover the sins of the people so that they could be in right standing with God.

Adam and Eve's choice to sin in the Garden of Eden means that all human beings are born into a sinful state. We are all guilty before God, and we have all sinned ourselves. Sin separates human beings from God. But under the New Covenant, Jesus made a sacrificial death on the cross for us. His sacrifice means that our sin is now completely removed, not just covered. Jesus is referred to as the Lamb of God—a perfect, sinless sacrifice. When we acknowledge our sin, ask forgiveness from God, and receive Christ as our Savior, we are then reconciled to God.

Remember, a single drop of Jesus' blood completely washes away all of your sin—even the sin of abortion. One drop of His blood atones for the bloodshed of every child who was ever aborted. It's that powerful. All we have to do is ask for and receive His forgiveness, and we are washed completely clean. Our guilt is removed.

Having another child because we're trying to make up for an abortion does not work. We don't need to atone for our sin, because Jesus Christ has already provided the only acceptable sacrifice for sin. It is not possible for any of us to make up for even the smallest sin we commit. Rather, we simply turn away from our sin, ask forgiveness, and put our faith in Jesus Christ. At that point, our sins are washed away forever by His blood. Our eternal spirits are born again, and God sees us as sinless and completely perfect through the blood of Jesus. He takes our sin away and gives us His righteousness in return.

Any actions we take to deal with the past—beyond receiving Christ as Savior—should not be thought of as attempts to atone for our sin. Our sin is atoned for by the blood of Christ, so any actions we take to deal with the past are simply ways that we seek to get our hearts, minds, and emotions in line with what is already true for our spirit being: that it is made new, perfectly righteous, completely healed and whole in Christ. Our actions cannot save our souls. Our goal should be to fully understand and receive Christ's perfect gift so that we can be free, healed, and whole. When we do that, we are able to help others and live the victorious and abundant life He has planned for us.

The point is, our works cannot save us. We have to make sure we fully understand this and get it deep down in our hearts. If we try to make atonement for our sins, we are failing to receive the finished work that Jesus did on the cross.

> But if we are living in the light, as God is in the light, then we have fellowship with each other, and the blood of Jesus, his Son, cleanses us from all sin.
>
> 1 John 1:7 NLT

Are you living in the light? Trying to carry our own guilt is a major way to continue wallowing in darkness. Gladly accept His free gift of forgiveness today. Don't walk in the darkness of guilt another minute! You are forgiven and cleansed.

While we do not, and indeed cannot, make up for the loss of our child, we do need to grieve the loss of our child. The grieving is for our healing, not for the purpose of making atonement. But the grieving process is crucial for post-abortive women, and we need to properly grieve not just the experience and the pain, but specifically the loss of our child.

That may seem obvious to some, but in my experience, not everyone understands this. Sometimes women do not realize that they need to grieve the loss of the child. It could be due to suppression of their feelings. There is also the issue that women continue to be told that there was not a baby inside them, but rather just a "blob of tissue" or a "clump of cells."

In 2016, some researchers at Northwestern University captured the moment of conception on camera, and found that a huge burst of light occurs at the exact moment a woman's egg is fertilized by the man's sperm cell.[2] From the moment we conceive, God is at work "knitting the baby together in the mother's womb." On the very first day of conception, "The first four cell divisions take place as the child travels down the mother's Fallopian tubes toward the uterus, all the while being nourished and protected by the mother's body."[3] Somewhere between 5 and 9 days after conception, the child is implanted in the mother's uterus. By day 21, the child has a circulatory system, brain, spinal column, and nervous system. By day 24, the child's heart is beating. By the fourth week, the child's heart is pumping the child's blood—with their own independent blood type—throughout his or her body.

Besides the clear science of the development process, every woman knows deep down that what is growing inside of her is a baby. If she carries to term, she won't give birth to a clock, or a dog, or a tree. The fruit of her womb was, is, and always will be a human being.

One lady I know of was raped at the age of 13 and conceived. Her parents decided that having an abortion was best due to the rape and the girl's young age. It was many years later before she realized she needed to grieve the loss of the child. Doing so enabled her to get to the root of many other issues in her life.

For me personally, I had certainly grieved the loss of my second child. That came naturally for me since I had wanted to have the baby. However, when I formally worked through the grief process during a support group, understanding everything better, it was then that I came to understand that I had another abortion in my past which needed to be acknowledged, and another child which needed to be grieved.

There are many cases I personally know of where it took the woman several years to come to terms with the fact that there was the loss of a baby due to their abortion. In the meantime, those women are often dealing with a loss of dignity and self-esteem. Because they haven't been able to come to terms with the reality of the situation, they have not properly healed yet.

One lady I encountered was feeling very sad because her youngest child had left home for college, which meant that she and her husband were empty nesters. Her mind quickly turned to thoughts of "if only" because she had aborted a baby after that child. Had she not done so, she and her husband would not be empty nesters. Because she had not properly acknowledged the loss of the child, grieved, and healed, feelings of regret, guilt, and sadness were still surfacing all of those years later.

Many common emotions and complications emerge as a result of both domestic abuse and abortion, but women often fail to recognize them as being brought on by grief associated with those sources. These may include guilt, shame, depression, sadness, anger, emptiness, anxiety, regret, insomnia, bitterness, numbness, mood swings, self-hatred, substance abuse, sexual dysfunction, and even suicidal tendencies.

Abortions often will bring to light any stress that was already prevalent in the relationship between the mother and father. The woman has now lost a baby to a cruel death that she was ultimately responsible for. However, she isn't "allowed" to mourn or feel any sorrow, because the premise of an abortion is supposed to be that the mother isn't doing anything wrong. Many women are told by their partners that they will leave them if they refuse an abortion. They feel that they have to choose between the baby and the partner. In an effort to save the relationship, she then complies. While the woman may have been trying to save the relationship by having an abortion, chances are now increased that the relationship's troubles will intensify, ultimately causing it to end. It's very common for uncommitted relationships to end quickly after an abortion.

Unmarried couples do sometimes stay together for a long period after an abortion, but it's the exception rather than the rule. Whenever that is the case, it is important for the man to come to terms with the part he played in the abortion. It will be more challenging for the woman to properly grieve and heal if her male partner stays stuck in the denial phase. Men experience many of the same emotions about abortion that women experience, but generally women are more in touch with their emotions. They also have a more direct experience in the case of abortion because it involves their physical body. For those reasons, it could prove more challenging for a man to come to terms with the need to grieve and heal.

Depression

When a woman comes to the realization that her abortion is a permanent and unchangeable act, sadness and depression usually set in. This could begin at any time—even many years later—after an abortion. For example, a woman might remain in the denial phase for many years, keeping feelings of sadness at bay or even buried deep down.

As with the others, there is no set period of time during which one should stay in this stage of grief. However, it's important to recognize that it can sometimes last for years, and this is of concern for several reasons. Feeling sadness over the loss of a child is a healthy part of the grief cycle. It's important to acknowledge our sadness and allow ourselves to experience those emotions before ultimately moving on to the next phase. On the other hand, a deep clinical depression is a serious condition that can be dangerous.

Depression often can lead to feelings of being stuck—not knowing how to move forward. Someone who is stuck in a serious, unhealthy phase of depression might experience any or all of the following problems: sleeping abnormally long hours of the day, isolation, feelings of being overwhelmed, feelings of hopelessness; intense guilt, regret, or shame; pessimism, loss of interest in things you used to enjoy; unending feelings of sadness or emptiness; suicidal thoughts or even attempts of suicide. If you have felt stuck in this kind of place for a long period of time, this is not a healthy place to be. Once you acknowledge the reality of what happened, seek God's forgiveness, and allow yourself to experience the emotion of sadness, you have adequately gone through the process. Your goal at that point should be to move toward the final phase, which is acceptance.

Some things that might help you move forward from the depression phase are seeing a medical doctor or seeing a counselor. Exercise and diet can help. There could be hormonal changes happening that a doctor can help with. And last, researchers are discovering more and more that gut bacteria or the "gut microbiome" plays a significant role in depression. That means prebiotic and probiotic foods and supplements could help significantly. Please see these videos on YouTube for more information: "Hidden Cause of Depression and Anxiety – Brain and Gut Connection – Dr.Berg" by Dr. Eric Berg DC, and "Try Lactobacillus Bifidobacterium for Depression – Natural Remedies for Depression – Dr.Berg" by Dr. Eric Berg DC.

Perhaps most importantly, God's Word has great power to bring change and inner healing. Find Scriptures about hope, joy, peace, and encouragement (openbible.info/topics/ is a great resource). Meditate on them and speak them over your life daily. You can and will come out of this.

Acceptance

When we first view the cycle of grief, we might make the mistake of thinking that getting to the acceptance phase is "the end." However, acceptance is still a stage of the grief cycle. Getting to that phase means getting to the beginning of a new phase. It also does not mean you are instantly and automatically done with all of the other phases.

What you should be aiming for at this point is that you

understand and accept that your life is now different than it was before. You cannot go back and change the past.

In the case of a situation of abuse, you certainly can and should change your future in the sense that you've gotten out of the abusive situation and you stay out of it. You can and should learn from your mistakes. But you cannot regain lost years or lost relationships.

In the case of abortion, you basically accept the reality of what has taken place, you receive God's forgiveness, and you begin to experience hope that there are better days ahead. Bad days may still happen, but you can and should expect that you will have many more good days than bad ones.

Healing Exercise: Getting Honest with the Lord

One of the first steps in working through our shock and denial phase is to get honest with the Lord. God wants to forgive you and heal you. He has already made provision for your forgiveness and healing by sacrificing Jesus on the cross. The next step is yours.

If you were underage, intimidated, emotionally manipulated, coerced, or physically threatened, or the physical safety of other loved ones was threatened, that means you do not carry the full responsibility for what happened. Other people carry some, most, or perhaps even all of the guilt in this sin.

Just to give a relevant analogy, think about children or young teenagers who are sold into sex slavery. They are committing sex outside of marriage. But because they are being forced to do that, no one would ever accuse them of sin. However, for many of us, the extent of the coercion we experienced still leaves us with some responsibility. To the extent we could have done more to stop what happened, we carry at least some responsibility.

So it's time to get honest with ourselves and with the Lord. If you are not sure whether or to what extent you may be guilty of sin, just ask the Holy Spirit to reveal it to you. Talk to a mature Christian who works to help others in this area. Ask them what they think.

If after praying and talking it over with a trusted minister or Christian counselor, you feel that you carry some or all of the responsibility for your abortion, then you need forgiveness and healing. In order to be completely forgiven, free, and healed, you have to forgive others, confess your own sin to God, and ask His forgiveness. Just say something like this:

> *Lord, I forgive all who were involved in making the decision to abort my baby. I choose to forgive all doctors, medical personnel and staff, all institutions and organizations, or anyone who was involved in any way during my abortion. I take responsibility for my part in the decision. I confess to You, Lord, that even though I felt afraid, threatened, or coerced, I ultimately chose to end my baby's life. This was wrong. It was a terrible sin, so I am coming to You for forgiveness. Will You please forgive me for ending my baby's life? I turn away from this sin, and I receive the forgiveness made available to me through the blood of Jesus Christ. Thank You, Lord, for Your forgiveness, mercy, and grace.*

God is not going to be surprised by your confession! He already knows what happened. He understands your pain.

Don't let guilt and shame drive you away from God. Let it drive you into His arms.

Be honest and sincere with Him. Share your heart and your emotions with Him. Let Him heal you. Ask Him to give you a deep and full revelation of His forgiveness, love, and acceptance of you.

Healing Exercise: Get a Stuffed Animal

One of the things I've done over the years when facilitating abortion recovery programs is to listen to a narrated version of the Frank Peretti book *Tilly*. The book is about a woman who dreamed she went to Heaven and while there, met the child she had aborted. If you've never read the book, I highly recommend it.

One Sunday afternoon, I got a phone call from a lady who had happened upon the book without knowing exactly what it was about and then read through the entire thing.

"Hello." She paused slightly then asked, "Is this Arlene?"

"Yes."

"My name is Sara. I got your name from the support group information at church."

"Hi, Sara. What can I do for you?"

Through gasping, tearful intervals, Sara began explaining the reason for her call. Following the church service that morning, she had wandered into the church bookstore and found a copy of *Tilly*. She recognized the author's name and had read some of his other books. She knew it was next to impossible to put a Frank Peretti book down, so she grabbed a copy. The book wasn't very big, so Sara figured she could easily read it in an afternoon.

This "chance" encounter with *Tilly* was actually a divine appointment because Sara had previously had an abortion, but had never dealt with it. *Tilly* brought all of Sara's repressed feelings of grief to light. As she concluded describing her dilemma to me, Sara asked, "What can I do?"

We had a lengthy conversation about the stages of grief, and I recommended for Sara to take several steps toward healing. One of those steps was to get a stuffed animal.

I was almost 45 years of age before I began the healing process for my abortions, and even at that seasoned stage of life, I needed comfort. There is something healing about having something soft and cuddly to hold. When your empty arms are aching for the baby that was ripped from you, you need something to cling to. I slept with a big cuddly snowman for several months during my depression phase. Mr. Snowman had a big, overstuffed rump which served a good purpose for me. I used to gently pat his bottom during intense moments of grief, just like a mother would with a real baby.

It may sound a little strange, but this significantly helped facilitate my healing.

Combating the Lies: Lie #6—You Are Stuck in One Stage of the Grief Cycle

Think back to the steps of the grief cycle: denial, anger, bargaining, depression, and acceptance. Examine your feelings. Where are you in the cycle?

Sometimes, we may be in one particular phase of the cycle for a very long period of time. When that happens, it's easy to feel like we are stuck—like we're trapped again, and we cannot get out. But that is not true.

God never intends for us to live permanently in a place of pain. There is a time to mourn, and a time to dance. A time to weep, and a time to laugh. Even if we have killed, God tells us that there is a time to heal.

> The One who breaks open the way will go up before them; they will break through the gate and go out. Their King will pass through before them, the LORD at their head."
>
> Micah 2:13 NIV

Wherever you feel stuck right now, you can make a choice to break out and move forward. God has the power to enable you to carry it out. You only need to make the choice. Just pray the prayer that corresponds to whichever phase of the grief cycle you find yourself in:

Denial: *Lord, I know that abortion is wrong. I cannot blame anyone else. Others may have influenced me, but I ultimately made the decision to end the life of my child. That is wrong, and I am sorry. Please help me to accept the reality of what I did, while also fully receiving and embracing your forgiveness and healing. Will you please forgive me for ending the life of my child? Will you please help me to heal from the damage my decisions have caused? Thank you, Lord.*

Anger: *Lord, I find myself deeply angry at people from my past. I recognize that there is righteous anger, but there is also unrighteous anger. Right now, I choose to lay my anger down at*

Your feet. I give it all to You. You decide what is righteous and what is unrighteous. If You want me to have any anger over abuse or abortion, I know You will send that anger back to me, but this time it will be wrapped in Your love.

Bargaining: *Lord, I understand that the decisions I made have consequences that will affect the remainder of my earthly life. However, it has been extremely difficult for me to accept those consequences. Please enable me to accept the fact that my baby is in Your hands. My baby is with You in Heaven, and because of Your blood shed for us on the cross, I will be reunited with my children one day in Heaven. Until that time, I will live for You here on this earth, serving You and doing Your will. In Jesus' name I pray, amen.*

Depression: *Lord, I know that it is not Your will for me to live in despair. The Bible tells me that You are near to the brokenhearted, and You save those who are crushed in spirit. My spirit is crushed, Lord. I need You to save me. I need You to comfort me. I need You to restore my soul. Right now, in the name of Jesus, I trade my mourning for the oil of joy. I embrace Your comfort as a product of Your goodness, not as something I have to earn or deserve. I ask You to sweep away this ash heap and put beauty in its place. In Jesus' name, amen.*

Acceptance: *Lord, I want to accept the past and move forward. Please enable me to accept the reality of my life as it is, not how it might have been. Help me to forget what is behind, and reach forward to the things that are ahead. In Jesus' name, amen.*

Discussion Questions

1. Are you experiencing grief in your life right now?
2. What phase of the cycle do you believe you are in?
3. After going through the chapter, including the exercises and prayers, do you still feel stuck or trapped in one of the grief stages?
4. Would you like someone else in the group to pray with you for freedom and healing?

SEVEN

Rebecca's Story

AT THE AGE OF FIFTEEN, Rebecca was very friendly and had an outgoing personality. Like most teenagers, she enjoyed going out to parties with her friends. People were drawn to her and that held true for members of the opposite sex.

During one particular party, she struck up a conversation with a young man named Robert. After a couple of beers, they decided to find a place where they could be alone and get to know each other better. That decision ultimately led them to the back seat of Robert's 1970 Dodge Dart Swinger.

At first, Rebecca welcomed Robert's kisses and advances. But after a short time, it escalated to a point beyond what she intended. Robert began touching her in places where she was not comfortable. Rebecca responded by repeatedly telling him, "No," and physically trying to resist. Robert did not let up, and ultimately raped Rebecca.

Like many young girls of her time, she did her best to brush this off as an unfortunate incident, but did not consider it worthy of pursuing with law enforcement or even with her parents. While being interviewed for the book, Rebecca explained, "At that time, both my parents and society, in general, seemed to have a mindset that might now be called victim shaming. Kind of like the old Toyota commercial said, 'You asked for it—you got it.' So people's attitude for something like this probably would have been, 'You were drinking out by yourself with a guy you barely knew—What did you expect? You made your bed, now lie in it.' The same attitude prevailed back then if a young woman got date-raped while wearing a miniskirt. Victims were often met with blame, shame, or indifference."

Instead of reporting the incident, Rebecca continued her party lifestyle, and a few months later, she went to Florida for spring break. Shortly after returning home to Michigan, she began to suspect that she was pregnant. She did not have a steady boyfriend, so if she was pregnant, that would mean that the father of her child was someone she barely knew—someone she had spent only a single night with just "for the fun of it."

The year was 1976, even though 2-hour tests had been available since 1970, Rebecca's doctor gave her a test that he said would take a couple of weeks before getting results back. In the meantime, he gave Rebecca some very strong antibiotics and told her that she had a bladder infection.

A couple of weeks later, when the doctor told Rebecca she was pregnant, he also told her that there was a good chance something was wrong with her baby—probably because of the antibiotics she had taken for a bladder infection.

So there are three obvious questions which come to mind

here: First, why would a doctor perform a pregnancy test that took two weeks to get back when accurate 2-hour tests were cheap and available? Second, why would he give Rebecca an antibiotic that was not safe for pregnant women, knowing that she had come there for a pregnancy test? And last, how would he have any way of knowing that something might be wrong with her baby's development that early in her pregnancy?

Rebecca's mother had a history of serious dysfunction. She was very manipulative. She was also a habitual liar, often making up or embellishing stories to get something she wanted. While Rebecca has no way to prove her suspicions, she now feels strongly that she knows what happened that day. Rebecca believes that after doing a normal 2-hour pregnancy test and discussing the results together, her mother and the doctor conspired with each other to coerce her into an abortion.

Indeed, the first place Rebecca and her mother were sent after Rebecca was given the "results" of her supposed pregnancy test was to Planned Parenthood. Even though their facility was 30 miles away, Rebecca was told she was being sent there for a consultation. The consultation was short and to the point—they wanted to "help" Rebecca by giving her an abortion. In fact, they even offered to help pay for it through donor money. They never once mentioned any other option to Rebecca, such as giving birth, parenting the baby, or putting the baby up for adoption.

While almost everyone else seemed to believe abortion was the best decision for her, Rebecca was not convinced. However, she had been raised in a home environment which did not tolerate any objection to parents. Her mom was adamant that she have an abortion, so Rebecca remained quiet about her concerns.

No one ever asked Rebecca what she wanted, or what she thought was the right decision. She had been given no say at all. Every arrangement was made for her, from the time of the first doctor's appointment. Rebecca felt that yes, she was young, but she also felt that the baby was hers and that this should be her decision to make.

As her mom drove her to the clinic, Rebecca knew that time was running out to voice her objections. She mustered the courage to tell her mother that she was having second thoughts about the abortion.

"You have made your decision," her mother immediately snapped. Although Rebecca knew that wasn't true, she also knew her mother well enough to know that this was just another one of her many lies and manipulations. Rebecca also suspected that her mom was trying to convince herself of this particular lie in an effort to ease her own conscience.

When they arrived, Rebecca noted the location as being a dark, colorless, shabby-looking brick building which housed several other businesses alongside the abortion clinic. As she lay on the table being prepped for the procedure, the nurse could sense that Rebecca was scared and hesitant. The nurse looked around and then quietly asked Rebecca, "Will you be okay?"

At that point, Rebecca was feeling very defeated. She knew that this might be a chance to back out, but she did not want to face the wrath of her mother. She took a deep breath and then slowly nodded her head in the affirmative.

After the procedure was over, Rebecca and her mother went back through a dreary hallway. At that point, Rebecca noticed that there was some kind of pro-life agency in the same building. In fact, it was only a few doors down from where her abortion had taken place. Rebecca had not noticed them on the way in, but she wondered why she had not been told to consult with them.

The drive home was marked by deafening silence, from the time they got in the car all the way until they pulled up in the driveway. Rebecca's head was spinning as she tried to process what had just happened. At the same time, she was still drowsy from the anesthesia. She recalls seeing her three siblings on the front porch, and then all of a sudden, the curt tone of her mother's voice broke through her thoughts with, "Go see your father."

Rebecca found her dad in his La-Z-Boy recliner, reading the newspaper. As she walked toward him, he got up, gave her a gentle hug, and then whispered, "Honey, I'm so sorry." Neither of them ever brought up the abortion to each other again.

As time passed, thoughts of the abortion began really bothering Rebecca. She decided to approach her mom about the struggle she was having. Once again, discussion was completely off the table, as her mother responded coldly, "You knew what you were doing."

Rebecca's mother lived in a world of her own lies.

Although Rebecca could not approach her mother about the abortion, she began to speak up about the issue to others whenever the opportunity presented itself. Rebecca understood that her abortion had been traumatic for her, so she became vocal about the damage it did to her.

Most of the post-abortive women I have encountered suffer in silence, especially those in our churches. Because of shame, guilt, or other pressures, they do not feel free to talk openly about their abortion experiences or their resulting struggles. But there are the ones who refuse to remain silent.

These women use their grief as a catalyst, and it becomes a driving force behind their voice. It is important for women and victims to speak out. However, as we covered previously, it is also important for those women to go through the healing process first. Once they do that, their anger becomes a righteous anger which can be used to draw others to God's love and forgiveness. When someone has anger over abortion without going through a healing process first, they can essentially become a "clanging cymbal" as described in 1 Corinthians 13, because they are not ultimately doing what they are doing from a place of love.

This is what happened to Rebecca early on. She was angry, and rightly so, because of what she had gone through. However, she didn't know anything about the grieving cycle or the process of healing.

Some months after her abortion, Rebecca became involved with a young man named Steve. She had known him from an early age, and he was a close friend of her cousin. Steve had been to Rebecca's house many times along with the cousin, and they would all hang out, play games, and have cookouts.

Now that Rebecca was officially old enough to date, it was a natural progression for her and Steve to become romantically involved. Rebecca shared with Steve about her abortion experience and he was very sympathetic. Steve was emotionally supportive—he felt sorrowful and compassionate toward Rebecca for what she had gone through. In fact, she had confided in him during her pregnancy and he had been the only one who encouraged her not to have an abortion. Steve had also met Rebecca's mother and knew firsthand how manipulative she could be. Rebecca felt angry about the situation, and Steve supported her right to feel angry.

When Rebecca graduated high school, she left home immediately and moved in with Steve. By now, they had been dating a couple of years and the relationship had experienced ups and downs. They had even had some rocky moments, but they went ahead and moved in together and shortly afterward got married. Then they moved to another state together. Once they were married and living away from family and friends, it wasn't long before a fight escalated enough that Steve hit her. Like many other women, Rebecca brushed it off. She believed him when he apologized and said it would never happen again.

A couple of months after that incident, Rebecca conceived. She lost that baby to a miscarriage, but within a few months, she was pregnant again. Four and a half months into this pregnancy, Rebecca found out that Steve was seeing another woman. Their relationship became off and on from that point. It also became more volatile, with Rebecca enduring two beatings during her pregnancy. In spite of the beatings, she gave birth to a healthy baby boy at full term.

Rebecca and Steve's relationship continued, as did the cycle of violence. At some point, they both moved back to their hometown separately, and their relationship continued to be on and off. About a year after the birth of her son, Rebecca became pregnant and endured another miscarriage. Almost two years after the birth of her son, Rebecca found out she was pregnant yet again. In light of the abortion and the miscarriages, she was very determined to have this baby. Emotionally, she did not feel that she could endure the loss of another child.

Now that she was pregnant again and back in her hometown, Rebecca went to see her family doctor—the same one her mother had taken her to see when she was 15. There were only two doctors in the small town where she lived, and she had heard a lot of complaints about the other doctor. Besides that, she had not yet realized that her family doctor had most likely conspired with her mother. She knew he had steered her toward abortion, but at this point in her life, she had not yet realized the full "scheme" that had been perpetrated by her mother and the doctor, so she ended up back at his office.

With indignation in her voice, Rebecca asked him point blank, "Is this one okay to have?" before following up with, "I will never do the abortion route again!"

Rebecca felt comforted and pleasantly surprised at his response: "And neither will I."

Apparently, this doctor had experienced a change of heart about abortion. This time, rather than giving her strong antibiotics, the doctor gave her his full support. Rebecca found out about some herbal remedies that were supposed to help prevent miscarriage, and she immediately began implementing them. Something worked, because she gave birth to a healthy daughter at full term.

Back when Rebecca was a young child, around the age of ten, her neighbor would frequently pick her up on Sunday mornings to attend church. Around that same age, she also enrolled in a Bible memory club and thoroughly enjoyed it. She recalls that the verses she memorized spoke to her heart, and she prayed to receive Jesus as her savior. As a teenager, she no longer attended church or pursued an active relationship with God. Even though she wandered her own way through her teenage and young adult years, she felt that those Bible verses and that experience never stopped being a part of her.

When her children were approximately five and seven years of age, Rebecca found herself returning to church every few weeks or so. Something about the experience was familiar and comforting, but the guilt and shame she felt for all of her past mistakes caused her to observe church at a distance. She would not attend every Sunday or get very involved. However, Steve was still abusive, so Rebecca's life became more and more unmanageable.

In fact, she began to feel that her life was spiraling out of control, and she knew deep down that turning to the Lord was the right answer. In spite of the conviction Rebecca felt, she still was not quite ready to give everything to the Lord. But she did attend church more and more frequently as time went on.

Everything changed when Rebecca's pastor did a series on the Apostle Paul, his life, and his ministry. Before Paul's conversion to Christianity, Paul hated Christians. He persecuted them and even led others in stoning Christians to death. As the study continued, Rebecca began to have a revelation that if God could change Paul from a murderer to a worshiper, He could do the same for her! Rebecca felt that she had also committed a murder when she had her abortion. She realized that she could be truly forgiven of this sin, and that God would not hold it against her at all. At that point, Rebecca fully embraced God's forgiveness and became a new person in Christ. She began to be more involved in church and even began attending a Christian college to study business and human resources management.

However, outside of her new life at church and college, Rebecca was still dealing with an abusive situation at home. Along the way, there had been many instances of Rebecca and Steve fighting, separating, and then reconciling. Steve wasn't a completely bad person. The hook Steve could always use to pull Rebecca back into himself was that he was always very supportive of Rebecca during times of crisis with her mother. Steve could see through the lies and manipulative moves Rebecca's mother would try to use against her, and his emotional support of Rebecca during those times was probably his strongest positive trait.

The final straw came late one afternoon during a heated dispute. After throwing some punches, pulling her hair, screaming at her, and chasing her around their apartment, Steve cornered Rebecca on the balcony. He was just about to throw her off, but Rebecca managed to somehow duck and run past him. The battle continued back inside, and in the midst of chasing Rebecca, Steve paused to catch his breath while leaning against a door.

As soon as he paused, Rebecca charged Steve like a raging bull. Steve was much bigger than Rebecca, standing exactly one foot taller than her. However, she grabbed him by his throat and lifted him up off the ground, pressing him up against the door. He hung there like a limp rag doll, terrified at what was happening since he knew that Rebecca could not have done this with her own natural strength.

They never had another physical altercation after that.

When Rebecca reflects back on that incident now, she

believes that either the Holy Spirit empowered her with strength as he did Samson, David, Benaiah, and other mighty warriors in the Bible. Or maybe it was a warring angel that came to help her fight, or maybe both. Either way, Rebecca's testimony always makes me think of the time I stood up to Louis and he later recognized the Holy Spirit in me.

After that last physical altercation, Rebecca and Steve separated again. A few months later, they reconciled. When they got back together, Steve never acted like he was about to raise a hand to her. Something had changed. He knew that there was an unseen force at work, and he could not deny its power. It seemed that Steve had learned his lesson. He understood that God does not look kindly on those who want to harm His children, and he had a healthy fear of harming Rebecca. Of course, this meant that Steve had lost his control over her.

The reconciliation seemed to be going well for a time, and Rebecca began thinking that maybe the relationship could work out well after all. Rebecca was now a couple of semesters from graduating the business program. However, during this reconciliation period, Steve asked Rebecca to drop out of college and move away with him. He had received a good job offer that was in another state. Rebecca wanted her family to be together, but she did not want to drop out of college, so she agreed to let Steve move with the kids, and then she would join them once she finished her degree.

Shortly before graduation, Rebecca's grandmother passed away. At the viewing, one of Rebecca's childhood friends came up and started chatting with her. They caught up on old times for a bit, and then Rebecca's friend started to make a reference to "Steve and Carla's. . ." A puzzled look came over Rebecca's face, and her friend stopped in mid-sentence.

Rebecca gathered herself and then responded, "Steve and Carla's *what*? Who is Carla?"

"Oh, I'm so sorry. I shouldn't have said anything . . . I thought you knew."

"Knew what? You have to tell me! You can't start something like that and not finish. I need to know—What are you talking about?"

After staring down at the floor for a moment, her friend looked up with a sad expression and said, "Steve and Carla's baby."

Obviously that changed everything. In retrospect, Rebecca believes that Steve wanting her to drop out of college was nothing but a control issue. He could see that she was getting to a place of independence, and he did not want to lose any more control over her. He knew that physical abuse was no longer an option, and he was losing the ability to control her mentally and financially too.

This, of course, was the final straw for Rebecca. She divorced Steve and never looked back.

Sometime after the divorce, Rebecca received counseling for the years of domestic abuse she had endured. Eventually she became involved in leading a support group for battered women at her local church, helping others find healing through the love of Jesus.

She also went through a support group for healing from abortion. That means she can now speak on the damage of abortion from a place of love rather than unrighteous anger.

Deliverance and Redemption Are Available to All

The revelation God gave Rebecca through the life of Paul is one that holds true for all of us. Before his conversion, Paul was known as Saul. Saul had been sincere in his beliefs, even as he was taking the lives of Christians. But he was sincerely wrong. So it is with many abortionists today. They believe they are helping a woman to exercise her "rights" over her body. They often view themselves as doing "what's best." My abortionist referred to the procedure as "helping me."

But the truth is that abortion is not a way of escaping pain or difficulty—it only leads to a different kind of entrapment.

Saul became so radically different that the Lord called forth his new identity by giving him a new name. This happened to several different people we find in the Bible. There was Abram, whom God renamed Abraham. Jacob became Israel. Simon became Peter. In biblical times, names were given to reflect some truth about a person's identity. A new name might denote a new relationship or a new phase of life. When we get to Heaven, it's possible that God is going to give each one of us a new name (see Revelation 2:17).

It is wonderful to think about how God saved Saul from himself. In reality, that's what we all need—to be saved from the damage caused by our wrong choices. The really good news is that God saves us *from* something *to* something else. And the "to" is always greater!

Acts chapter 19 describes Saul's encounter with God, explaining that the light from Heaven struck him with such force that it knocked him off of the donkey he was riding. For some reason, whenever I read about that encounter I can't help but laugh a little. I'm not completely sure why. Maybe it's the picture generated in my imagination that seems funny. However, I also quickly reflect on the fact that God has a plan to knock each one of us off of our donkey, and that's not funny.

God has a way of turning our eyes to Him. Sometimes it will be through a trauma, as it was for me. God is loving and it's not necessarily that He sends the trauma, but He will use difficult experiences to get our undivided attention. Trauma can serve a purpose, and God can use difficulty to strengthen us. Yes, sometimes we feel we have reached our breaking point. We feel like we cannot take anymore. But God's grace is sufficient to see us through. He also promises that we won't ever have to take a sinful way out of any situation—He always provides a way of escaping temptation (see 1 Corinthians 10:13). That means He has a better solution!

Sometimes, there is a "suddenly" moment that happens in our lives. Our spiritual eyes are opened to some profound and life-changing truth about God, as was the case for Saul. Luke chapter 24 gives us another example with the two men who walked on the road to Emmaus. Jesus walked with them for a while and had in-depth conversations with them, and they did not recognize that it was him. That is, until their eyes suddenly opened.

We do not know when or how our deliverance from the painful situation will occur. But it will happen in the Lord's timing. He does see you in your pain, and He will make a way of escape. He is your Deliverer!

The Lord will orchestrate a deliverance for you and your circumstances. The current pain you are experiencing will not last forever.

Your deliverance probably won't come through the same mechanism that mine did. It probably won't come the same way Rebecca's or Jill did. But it will come. I don't know how it will come, but I know that God is faithful.

Sometimes God delivers us from danger, and sometimes He takes us through it. In the case of Peter, God sent an angel to walk him right past guards and straight out of prison. Literal chains fell from his hands as he gained his freedom. But he did have to stand up and be obedient to follow the angel out of the prison. That probably took some courage. Whatever God sends your way, whatever open door He provides you, please be wise enough to take it!

As I have worked with abused women over the years, I've seen many instances of God providing a way out of their situation, but the woman refusing to walk through that door because of fear. Believe me, I understand the fear. I understand the emotional and mental enslavement. But if the Lord is giving you a way out, He's also going to protect you while you're walking out of your prison. There might be challenges along the way, but when God gives you a door, you must go!

Making the Right Choices Can Start Today

While interviewing Rebecca for the book, I asked her for the main lesson she would like readers to take away from her story. Her answer was, "Do not live with or marry an unbeliever."

> Do not be yoked together with unbelievers. For what do righteousness and wickedness have in common? Or what fellowship can light have with darkness?
>
> 2 Corinthians 6:14 NIV

Rebecca also said that she would like for people to understand that often, the abused woman is suffering in silence, but would likely be receptive to someone reaching out. Looking back, Rebecca wishes that just one person would have made an attempt to reach out and intervene in her situation, but no one ever did. She wishes that someone would have tried to talk to her, offer assistance, or just ask questions and listen to her.

She also imagines other ways people could have helped. "Maybe one person praying in front of the abortion clinic might have made a difference. Maybe one person holding a sign might have caused me to reconsider."

I have often looked back and had similar thoughts. Maybe one person saying, "You don't have to do this," might have made a difference.

God Has Dealt with Cruelty and Pain

Each post-abortive woman has her own unique story. Certain themes come up repeatedly, such as affairs, sexual promiscuity, career considerations, finances, age, health, and so on. But the bottom line for all of us is that we gave up our babies to a cruel death that they did not deserve. On the flip side, when we have experienced abuse, we have suffered in many ways we did not deserve.

Here is the good news: Jesus Himself was abused. He never did anything wrong. Not a single thing. He was perfectly loving to every human being He ever met, yet His body was torn to shreds. He was mocked and insulted. They spat in His face and beat Him. Then they pounded spikes into His hands and feet and hung Him naked on a cross until He died. He knows what it's like to suffer abuse at the hands of wicked people.

Because He suffered in those ways, you can live. You can be healed. You can forgive your abusers, just like Jesus did. As He hung on the cross, He prayed, "Forgive them, Father, for they know not what they do."

It was out of His love for us that He endured these things.

However, death did not defeat Him. He rose from the dead, completely healed, restored, and victorious. And He offers us that same victory today.

Open your heart to Jesus and let Him do His healing work. We are approaching the final stretch of a journey that probably seemed very uncertain when we began. But you've come this far, and you're doing a great job. You have made tremendous progress in developing understanding about the issues you've been through in your life. The next step is to embrace the healing power of Jesus Christ. Are you ready?

> I have heard your prayer and seen your tears; I will heal you.
>
> 2 Kings 20:5 NIV

Combating the Lies: Lie #7—Your Sin Requires You to Be Punished

If an abortion occurs before an abusive relationship, we may subconsciously think we need to be punished for our sin. We put out a silent radar to attract abusive partners and toxic relationships, or we may even unwittingly seek them out ourselves. Deep down, the guilt we carry in our hearts is driving us, and our hidden motive goes something like this, "I deserve to be punished for taking the life of my baby, so it's okay for me to be abused. This is what I deserve."

While there are always consequences for sin, God is not up there dealing out punishment to you via an abusive partner. Every human being deserves eternal punishment for sinning against God, but Jesus Christ already took our punishment on Himself! God has no interest and no agenda to dole out a second punishment for sins that His Son already died for. Please read this passage and note the words emphasized in bold:

> For everyone has sinned; we all fall short of God's glorious standard. Yet God, in his grace, freely makes us right in his sight. He did this through Christ Jesus when **he freed us from the penalty** for our sins. For God presented Jesus as the sacrifice for sin. People are made right with God when they believe that Jesus sacrificed his life, shedding his blood. This sacrifice shows that God was being fair when he held back and **did not punish those who sinned** in times past, for he was looking ahead and including them in what he would do in this present time. God did this to demonstrate his righteousness, for he himself is fair and

just, and **he makes sinners right in his sight** when they believe in Jesus.

Can we boast, then, that we have done anything to be accepted by God? No, because our **acquittal** is not based on obeying the law. It is based on faith.

Romans 3:23-27 NLT, emphasis added

Penalty. Punishment. Acquittal. These are the words God uses to describe what He did for us through Jesus. We all deserved punishment. We all deserved to pay a penalty. But Jesus Christ paid our penalty for us. He took our punishment. It is over. "It is finished"—as Jesus put it. Come down off of your cross and stop punishing yourself. Fully receive and embrace what He has done for you!

Discussion Questions

1. Have you experienced manipulations and lies? Did it cause you to become a victim, and if so how?
2. If you were a victim of abortion, were you coerced to do so?
3. Have you experienced betrayal in your life?
4. Can you think of a time when you were saved from something?

Conclusion

STAYING FREE

There are certain keys to full recovery, restoration, and healing. We have touched on them in previous chapters, but the process of freedom and healing is one that requires serious effort. It's crucial to be thorough in working through issues. We don't have to fear staying trapped. God delights to set us free. But we need to be diligent in doing our part.

We must repent of (meaning "to turn away from") all secrecy. Again, that does not mean we have to go telling everyone our deepest, darkest secrets. Sure, God may use some of us down the road to share our testimonies for the purpose of comforting, encouraging, and inspiring others. But for now, the focus is on making sure that we are completely free and healthy.

Think about how we deal with physical wounds like cuts. We may cover it with a bandage for a time in order to keep germs and debris out, but there comes a time when it needs to be exposed to light and air. In the same way, our secrets

Conclusion

need to see the light of day in order for us to experience complete healing.

Satan always works in the dark. His tools are deceptions, underhanded schemes, and various forms of subterfuge. Confessing our secrets openly to another believer strips the enemy of his power. Imagine if you were able to take an enemy's weapons and turn them back around to use against that enemy. This is what confession does for the believer!

When we confess our secrets to another believer, they can bathe our wounds with prayer and the light of God's Word. God can then begin to use our past hurts for good. However, if we remain shrouded in the dark clouds of secrecy, we will continue to be a victim of the enemy. Don't fall for that trap! You've been victimized enough in your life!

If you are still living with any form of domestic violence, you need to hear yourself confessing that truth out loud. You need to hear yourself say these words out loud, "I am being abused."

Doing that will help bring you out of denial. It also puts the enemy on notice that his power over you is broken, and he better start moving on down the road because he is losing his grip on you. He is being exposed.

You also need to develop a network of support so that you can successfully come out of the abusive situation once and for all. The importance of communication, emotional support, and networking cannot be overstated.

Just to give you an example, one time I got a telephone call at work. It was my church's secretary. I was quite surprised to hear from her since she had never called me before at all, much less at work. She explained, "I have an Aurora police officer sitting in my office right now. One of the battered women you work with here at the church is missing. Her family is trying to track her down. Do you have any idea where she might be?"

Those words still send a chill down my spine.

The only clue I had was to recall that she was getting pretty close with one of the other members of our group. They had developed a friendship. I gave them that lady's name and the authorities contacted her. She was not with her friend from the group, but her friend was able to give the police information that allowed them to successfully locate the missing woman.

Continue Refuting the Lies and Clinging to Truth

When my relationship with Louis ended, one of his parting shots was to declare, "You never tried to make this relationship work." In effect, he was taking one last opportunity to say, "This is all your fault."

If he could have gotten me to believe that lie, maybe he would have been able to maintain some power in my life. But an objective look at the facts proved him wrong. I had to examine this accusation and know that it was a lie.

The truth was that I did everything I possibly could to try to appease Louis so that we could have a relationship. I allowed myself to be cut off from my family and friends. Living with a man outside of marriage was against my religious beliefs, but that's what Louis wanted, so I consented to this for years. None of these things were healthy or right or good, but it is clear that I was doing whatever I possibly could to try to make the relationship work. There's no way he was going to tag me with one last dart on his way out. This was nothing but another lie.

During my healing process, I was at a Silent Voices weekend retreat. One major principle I learned there was, "Tell yourself the truth!" The words and tapes we play in our heads affect us. The truth is what God says about you. What another person says, what the enemy says, these get exposed by God's Word. Stay in God's Word daily and do not let the enemy tell you anything different from what God's Word tells you.

Naming Your Baby

One of the major steps in healing from abortion is to give your baby a name. This serves several purposes. First, giving your baby a name acknowledges the humanness of your baby. This is a way to refute the lie that your baby was only a "clump of cells" or a "product of conception." This act helps to bring us out of denial.

It's wise to pray about the name. During prayer, the Lord might impress upon you what sex your child is. If he doesn't do that, you must not beat yourself up about it. You've taken enough beatings in your life. If you don't have any idea what sex your child is, you can just choose a gender-neutral name like Aiden, Amari, Ashton, Devon, Jayden, Jaylen, Jaime, Jody, Jordan, Kendall, Morgan, Reese, Riley, Robin, Sawyer, Skylar, or Taylor (just to name a few).

After you acknowledge their humanness by giving your baby a name, it's a good idea to write them a letter. This letter gives you an opportunity to say whatever you would like to say to your child. You may want to tell them how deeply sorry you are. You may want to talk about the reasons why you chose an abortion, or to describe the circumstances surrounding your decision. You might simply choose to write about lighter content like telling them about their siblings, your life here on earth, and how you are excited to one day meet them in Heaven.

It's your baby and your letter. Your choice.

The letter is an exercise to help you heal. The Bible doesn't tell us exactly what people in Heaven can or can't see about what happens on the earth after they leave. Since the Bible describes those who have gone before us as "a great cloud of witnesses," many believe that they can see at least some of what happens. What we know for sure is that God forbids praying to, or otherwise trying to communicate directly with, human beings who have passed on from this life. To try to communicate with the dead through some "spiritual" exercise or method is called "necromancy" and God tells us that it is wrong and dangerous. So the letter really is an exercise in healing and not an attempt to actually communicate with your child. Can your child see the letter, or anything going on in your life right now? We don't know for sure.

What is certain, however, is that if you have received Jesus Christ as Savior, you will one day be reunited with your child in Heaven. At that point, I imagine that this letter will have special meaning to both of you. Again, these decisions are totally up to you. There is no right or wrong method, and anyone who tells you anything other than what has been stated here better have some incredibly clear scriptural proof to back up their assertions. Loving, gentle, biblical correction and guidance are good and healthy, but there is no place for anger, harshness, judgment, adding things to Scripture, or condemnation toward a woman who is seeking to heal from abortion.

Another choice that is totally up to you is whether or not you will share your letter with any human being. Either way, I would suggest saving the letter for a couple of reasons. One reason is that down the road, long after you have completely healed, you might come to a point of wanting to share your letter with other women in order to help them heal. Even if you can't imagine doing that right now, it could happen down the road.

Second, I personally find it helpful to go back through every once in a while and read the letter again. This is not to keep us dwelling on grief. Rather, the purpose is to be able to see and understand how much God has healed us. Down the road, does the letter still stir up raw emotion? If so, there might be some area where we still need healing. On the other hand, even after we are completely healed, the letter will likely bring a bittersweet kind of feeling—one of missing your child, while at the same time knowing they are healed and whole and perfectly safe in the Lord's arms.

Envisioning Your Child

My abortions were many years ago. When I first began the healing process, I used to envision my children as babies. As the years have gone by and I have healed, I have pictured them growing up, and I now picture them as a handsome grown man and a lovely lady.

However, we may not have to mourn the loss of experiencing our babies growing up years. We simply don't know for sure what God has in store for us in Heaven. On a recent episode of *The 700 Club*, a lady named Charlotte Holmes shared her testimony of experiencing Heaven when her earthly body was clinically dead in a hospital for 11 minutes.[1]

Generally, we need to be discerning about testimonies involving near death experiences. The ones that are verifiable medically, agree with the Bible, and glorify Jesus Christ are likely to be genuine, whereas any that do not agree with the truth of the Bible are rightly classified as counterfeits. Charlotte is a Christian, and her testimony agrees with the Bible and gives glory to Jesus Christ.

There are several interesting aspects of Charlotte's testimony, but most relevant for us is the fact that Charlotte had experienced a miscarriage 48 years prior to her near death experience. She explains of her heavenly visit, *"I saw a toddler, and that toddler—I couldn't understand. And I remember thinking, 'Who is this?'*

And I heard my heavenly Father say to me, 'It's your child.'

I had lost that child. I was five and a half months pregnant. I can remember them holding the baby up and saying, 'Charlotte, it's a boy.' Then he was gone.

So when I'd seen this toddler, I said, 'God, how's that possible?'

He says, 'They continue to grow in Heaven, but there's no time. It's eternity.'

So 48 years later, and here my child, our child, is a toddler."

Letting Go

Now that you can acknowledge that your baby was more than a clump of cells or "product of conception," you have

Conclusion

given humanness to your child by naming the baby and writing them a letter. As previously mentioned, there is no tangible body or precious memories to hold onto. You have gone through a grief process, and it is now time for closure to say goodbye. For that reason, many retreats or Bible studies conclude by having a memorial service. I have been to several different ones over the years. Every service is different, but the following are some suggestions for how you or your group might go about having one.

Certainly there should be a quiet setting. Most services have dim lighting and soft music playing in the background. The songs might be lullabies or songs of comfort. Or perhaps just soothing instrumentals.

Some services allow the participants to bring a guest with them.

The facilitator of the group or retreat will usually say some words of comfort, compliment the participants on the difficult work they have done, read some scripture, and maybe say a prayer out loud.

Frequently there is a table in the front of the room with unlit candles. Participants will take turns lighting the candles in memory of their little one. If the participant has had more than one abortion, she will light the appropriate number of candles. Sometimes there may be a little card with the baby's name on it.

Some services will have the participants holding a doll or some kind of stuffed animal that they have been given. Often there will be some kind of special lullaby sung or played. There are various songs that can be done in remembrance. One of my favorites is *Jesus Has a Rocking Chair* by the Greenes.

A lot of times the grieving mothers will be given a chance to say a few words if they choose to do so. Sometimes each participant will be given a rose or a small bouquet of flowers. Something to make her feel special, and worthy of motherhood.

Another idea is to have the service proceed outside with a balloon release, perhaps with the child's name on it. I have known some to plant a tree as a group, or trees individually, in remembrance of the babies.

There is no right or wrong way to do a service. And it will help bring closure, healing, and peace to mothers of aborted babies. I have never seen an abortive mother have a memorial service for her baby without it being deeply and profoundly meaningful to her.

Abortion Recovery Retreats

You may be doing this book as part of a group study, and if so, that's wonderful. Keep going. However, I would also like to recommend retreats that are designed to help women heal from abortion, such as Silent Voices, Rachel's Vineyard, and Deeper Still. Many pro-life crisis pregnancy centers will also offer Bible studies and other types of support groups. You don't have to live in this phase of life forever, but you do want to be thorough in making sure you are healed. Besides going through the healing process, you can also make wonderful friendships with the women you meet there.

Sometimes, particular aspects of our healing can be more of a process than a single event. For example, we may have a good head knowledge of the fact that we are forgiven, but still carrying some guilt deep down in our hearts.

Conclusion

If you are wondering whether you might still be carrying guilt, let's think through some questions. How would you describe yourself today in the context of this issue? Would you say that you have committed an abortion? Would you consider yourself to be a killer? A murderer?

Abortion is a terrible sin, and the goal is not to deny it. However, when you are in Christ, your identity is now in Him. Your sins have been washed away, and they do not define who you are. You are not a sinner. You're a new creation in Christ! You're saved. Redeemed. You are now part of the family of God.

This is just one example of God's truth that we need to get deep into our hearts. This is what allows us to know that we are completely healed and whole, when there is no longer any part of us that is struggling to fully receive and walk in the forgiveness and grace of Jesus Christ.

If you are sure you're completely healed, you may not need an abortion retreat. However, I don't believe that going to one will hurt you, and it is very likely to help.

Forgiving Those Who Have Hurt You

Forgiveness is sometimes more of a process. Yes, we make the choice to forgive. However, many times the pain, the thoughts, and the memories will linger. If you find yourself struggling to move beyond the painful memories of abuse, you might try writing a letter to your abuser. This is a letter that you will not send.

Do not try to contact a past abuser.

Rather, this is simply an exercise to work through your feelings, give them to God, and experience closure.

You can write out the letter by "telling" your abuser what they did to you. "Confront" them with the reality of it. Then tell them how all of those things made you feel and how they affected you.

Last, tell them that you forgive them. Tell them you release them of the debt they owe you, and you hope they find their own forgiveness, healing, and peace.

Forgiving Ourselves

The Bible does not explicitly reference forgiving one's self. Since the biblical concept of forgiveness is absolution of a debt that is owed, it doesn't really apply to ourselves in the same way it does to others. A person cannot owe a debt to themselves, after all.

But what happens is that we do continue trying to punish ourselves, even after we have gone through all the motions of asking God for His forgiveness. Essentially what is happening is that we're still trying to pay our own debt. The only true payment for sin happened on the cross. People who choose to forego that provision end up being cast into Hell for eternity, because a human being cannot ever fully pay the debt. It's eternal.

But in our minds and hearts, we still feel like we should be doing something to make up for what we did—some kind of penance or punishment or striving to earn God's mercy. We can't do it. It's not possible.

The only possibilities for human beings in regard to this issue are: 1) Fully receive God's forgiveness by what Jesus did on the cross 2) Ultimately reject His sacrifice for us. When we try to earn God's forgiveness, we are declaring that

Conclusion

the cross isn't enough. The concept is quite ridiculous. It's akin to Jesus paying off a multi-trillion-dollar debt for us, and then us spending the rest of our lives working and striving for a few pennies to throw in after Him.

Stop punishing yourself. It is an affront to what Jesus did for you on the cross. He gave His life for you. Receive what He did for you. Let yourself off the hook. Stop striving. Stop trying to earn His mercy. You can't, and you don't have to. Let His love flood into your soul. Put your full trust in His blood. It is sufficient to pay for all of your sins!

Prayer

Lord, I let myself off the hook today. I no longer want to punish myself for the past. I completely receive your forgiveness and grace, and I choose not to hold anything against myself any longer. Your Word says that who the Son sets free is free indeed. Thank You for setting me free. I receive Your freedom, in Jesus' name, amen.

Accepting the Past

God never needs anyone's forgiveness because He has never done anything wrong. He is morally perfect. Everything He does is loving and good and right. We may not understand that right now, but we can at least mentally consent to the fact that it is true. We can also rest in the fact that we will understand more completely when we get into eternity.

If a person feels that they need to "forgive" God, what's probably happening is that they feel like God wasn't there for them. They were abused or hurt and they don't understand why God didn't stop those things from happening. Here's what we must realize. God created a world where human beings have a choice between good and evil. Sometimes they choose good and sometimes they choose to do what is evil. If God zapped every person off the face of the earth before they committed an act of evil, none of us would be here for very long!

God's goodness does not require Him to step in and thwart every act of evil before it takes place. One day soon He is going to end all evil, but we aren't there yet. Right now, God is still allowing good and evil to fight for the souls of humankind so that more people can be saved and He can complete His work on this current version of earth. What that means for us is that evil does take place. However, God does not do evil. Everything He does is right and good, and we must acknowledge this. We must receive that truth into our hearts.

Once we do that, we must then give up our need for the past to have been different from what it was. Rather than forgiving God, we need to give up our own ideas about what God should or should not have done. He is always good, no matter what. This is an issue that we all must settle firmly in our hearts.

Prayer

Lord, I want to move with You beyond the past. I let go of my need for the past to have been different from what it was. I acknowledge that You are completely and perfectly

Conclusion

good and righteous, and I release You from any debt that I have felt You owed me. You do not owe me anything. Let's please move forward together. In Jesus' name I pray, amen.

Knowing You Are Healed

Years ago, I found myself crying as I thought about my past abuse and abortions. However, unlike all the many times before, these tears were not tears of guilt, shame, or grief. Instead, I was crying tears of thankfulness and joy. I knew that I had been forgiven and healed. There was so much gratitude inside of me for Jesus, my Savior. He had done so much for me!

However, the tears of joy also started getting mixed with tears of compassion. I thought about all the many women still locked in their prisons of pain, and my heart longed for them to be free.

My heart longs for you to be free today. Hopefully this book has helped a great deal in regard to you finding freedom and healing. However, no single book, program, or experience is perfect. If you feel that you still need some level of freedom or healing, I would encourage you to persevere until you get there. I promise, it is worth the effort.

Resources

- National Domestic Violence Hotline (United States) 1-800-799-SAFE (7233) or 1-800-787-3224 (TTY)
- National Domestic Violence Hotline (Canada) 1-800-363-9010
- http://www.troubledwith.net, A website of Focus on the Family – Answers questions about family, relationships, depression, and domestic abuse.
- https://verbalabusejournals.com, A website focusing on verbal and emotional abuse; includes a safety plan.
- https://lundybancroft.com, Lundy Bancroft's website. Includes a great list of resources for many types of abused women.
- http://cryingoutforjustice.wordpress.com, Pastor Jeff Crippen's website focusing on spiritual abuse in the church.

- https://whengeorgiasmiled.org, Dr. Phil & Robin McGraw's website.
- https://www.shefoundhisgrace.org, Serena Dyken's website includes post-abortion classes and resources.
- https://herchoicetoheal.com, Sydna Masse's website offers online post-abortion healing and information.
- https://afterabortion.org, David Reardon's website. Information on abortion risks, complications, research, abortion recovery, and educational materials.
- Many local Crisis Pregnancy Centers offer post-abortion resources and the Forgiven and Set Free Bible study.

WEEKEND RETREATS

- Rachel's Vineyard – https://www.rachelsvineyard.org
- Silent Voices – Sharon Pearce's retreat – https://silentvoices.org
- Deeper Still – https://www.pregnancyresourcecenter.org

BOOKS

- Jeff Crippen and Anna Wood, *A Cry for Justice: How the Evil of Domestic Violence Abuse Hides in Your*

Church (United States: Calvary Press Publishing, 2012)
- Jane Brennan, *Motherhood Interrupted: Stories of Healing and Hope After Abortion* (United States: Xlibris Corporation, 2008)
- David C. Reardon, *The Jericho Plan: Breaking Down the Walls Which Prevent Post-Abortion Healing* (Acorn Books, 1996)
- Frank E. Peretti, Tilly: *A Novel* (Crossway Books, 1998)
- Theresa Burke, *Forbidden Grief: The Unspoken Pain of Abortion* (Acorn Books, 2002)

Notes

Introduction

1. https://www.jpands.org/vol22no4/coleman.pdf
2. https://www.thedailybeast.com/coerced-abortions-a-new-study-shows-theyre-common
3. https://thehill.com/changing-america/respect/equality/585169-homicide-is-a-leading-cause-of-death-in-pregnant-people
4. http://www.stopforcedabortions.org/docs/ForcedAbortions.pdf

2. Broken and Mended

1. https://www.guttmacher.org/sites/default/files/pdfs/pubs/journals/socscimed201002009.pdf
2. See here for more information about this problem: https://www.liveaction.org/news/forced-abortion-ultimate-form-domestic-violence/
3. See here for details about a recent study: https://www.pop.org/many-american-women-felt-pressured-abortions-study-finds/

4. The Dynamics of Domestic Violence

1. https://hbr.org/2013/03/the-ideal-praise-to-criticism Accessed 8-31-21
2. https://www.womenshealth.gov/relationships-and-safety/domestic-violence/effects-domestic-violence-children Accessed 8-31-21
3. https://www.parents.com/pregnancy/everything-pregnancy/another-heartbreaking-way-domestic-violence-affects-children-even/ Accessed 8-31-21
4. https://www.baptiststandard.com/opinion/voices/abuse-is-biblical-grounds-for-divorce/

5. The Tie That Binds

1. https://youtu.be/T_nOvCIpkIQ THE HIDDEN COST OF SOUL TIES, RC Blakes, Jr, Uploaded August 15, 2016
2. Dutton, Donald & Painter, S.L.. (1981). Traumatic bonding: The development of emotional attachments in battered women and other relationships of intermittent abuse. Victimology. 6. 139-155.

6. Understanding the Grieving Process

1. Graphic source: https://www.gvsu.edu/counsel/grief-and-loss-week-two-335.htm
2. https://www.liveaction.org/news//scientists-say-life-begins-at-conception-with-flash-of-light/
3. https://www.hli.org/resources/miracle-fetal-development/

Conclusion

1. https://www.youtube.com/watch?v=4JUb8Zw7ucw

Acknowledgments

I am grateful to so many people:

Pam Koerbel, whose book helped me see how wounded I was and started me on my healing journey. Your work was not in vain and continues through those of us you helped with your encouraging words. You are now in a far better place.

Kathy and Joy, who were the first women to begin walking me through the healing process. Also to Sharon Pearce of Silent Voices, whose repetitive statement of, "Tell yourself the truth!" still rings in my ears from many years ago.

Rebecca and Jill, whose stories I pray will help others heal.

Pastor Debbie Stafford, for the training, opportunity, and trust so many years ago in learning about domestic violence.

R.C. Blakes, a man who I have not had the privilege of

meeting, but who gave me permission to use valuable information on soul ties. God bless you!

David Reardon, for your years of research and work in proving that abortion is not a safe, simple, and quick procedure, and for helping to bring to light the vast array of problems and complications resulting from it. It does not go unnoticed, nor does your friendship.

Allan Parker, who has worked tirelessly to bring justice to the nation in fighting for those in the womb who cannot speak. Thank you, thank you, for giving the many women (and men) a platform to speak of the devastation abortion has brought to their lives. Many thanks to my sisters at Operation Outcry for their deeply valued friendships and support.

My niece, Vicki, who helped her technologically challenged aunt through various stages of computer learning! Also, my niece Deb, who kept this project covered in prayer for so long and to Deb's husband, Allen, for his publishing experience advice.

Coach Tamra, who kept encouraging me through the many times I wanted to give up. The words of "so many people need this" are still fresh in my ears. Also, the Steve Harrison team for endless hours of teaching about the world of writing and publishing, of which I knew nothing! A special thanks to Coach Cristina for her teaching and support, and the "authority of authors" as Geoffrey says of my GPN family.

Chris and Shannon McKinney, who believed in my message and found it valuable enough to spend endless hours editing, formatting, and designing the cover—and for having the faith that this work needs to be published. This dream would not have come true without you!

Anyone who read and gave input before publishing, and all who prayed and supported in any way whom I haven't named. You know who you are. More importantly, God knows. May you be richly rewarded.

Finally, and most importantly, my Lord and Savior Jesus Christ who planted this idea in me a long time ago. This is His book, not mine.

Publisher's Note: An Invitation to Paradise

All of us wonder why there is pain in the world. We struggle with questions like, "Why would a good God allow so much suffering?" When we ask that question, what we're effectively saying is, "Why doesn't God do something?" We struggle to understand why He doesn't step in and put an end to human suffering once and for all.

The reality is, He is going to do that very thing. One day, He will physically step back into the scene. He is going to put His foot on the Mount of Olives in Jerusalem, and begin the process of restoring earth to its former glory and perfection. The Bible describes the future earth this way:

> Then I saw "a new heaven and a new earth," for the first heaven and the first earth had passed away, and there was no longer any sea. I saw the Holy City, the new Jerusalem, coming down out of heaven from God, prepared as a bride beautifully dressed for her husband. And I heard a loud

> *voice from the throne saying, "Look! God's dwelling place is now among the people, and he will dwell with them. They will be his people, and God himself will be with them and be their God. 'He will wipe every tear from their eyes. There will be no more death' or mourning or crying or pain, for the old order of things has passed away."*
>
> *He who was seated on the throne said, "I am making everything new!"*
>
> Revelation 21:1-5 NIV

No more tears. No more pain.
The world that we all long for is coming.
It's on the way.
The big question is: Will you be part of that new world?

In order to be part of that new world, we must receive Jesus Christ as Lord and Savior. There will be pleasures beyond anything we can imagine in that new world. In fact, one of the first things we will experience there is a huge party called, "The Wedding Feast of the Lamb." There will be wine, music, dancing, celebration, and immense joy.

But there will not be any rebellion against God.

The only people who will be in God's new world will be the ones who chose to love Him and give their lives to Him. Just like Jesus asked His disciples, "Who do you say that I am?" we must all answer that same question.

Who Is Jesus?

God the Father sent His One and Only Son, Jesus Christ, to this imperfect world to redeem us and restore us into a free and open relationship with Himself. Because humankind had sinned, our relationship with God was broken. Severed. And we were under the penalty of sin, which is punishment and death.

Instead of leaving us to suffer those penalties, Jesus decided to take our place. He took our punishment for us by dying a gruesome death on the cross. Jesus was then buried, and on the third day, He was resurrected into eternal life. He defeated death and the grave, and that means we can now freely receive forgiveness for all of our sins.

God's Offer to Everyone

Eternal life with God in His perfect world is offered to all of us.

If we choose to reject this offer, that means we are choosing sin over God. We are choosing to stay in rebellion toward Him. This will be the result for those who choose to stay in rebellion toward God:

> "But the cowardly, the unbelieving, the vile, the murderers, the sexually immoral, those who practice magic arts, the idolaters and all liars—they will be consigned to the fiery lake of burning sulfur. This is the second death."
>
> Revelation 21:8 NIV

Publisher's Note: An Invitation to Paradise

When presented with options in life, we all want to make the best decision. We weigh all of our important decisions, and we choose carefully.

You can make the right choice today. At this very moment, you are being given the option to end your rebellion toward God, turn away from sin, and choose to receive His forgiveness. You can choose right now to receive Christ as Savior.

A Prayer for Salvation

If you want to receive Christ as Savior, here is a prayer you can pray right now:

God, I want to live in Heaven with You forever. I do not want to live in sin and rebellion. No human being is perfect, including me. I have done things that You say are wrong. Please forgive me of all my sins, and please give me a new life with You. I now receive Jesus Christ as my Lord and Savior.

Thank you, God, for saving me!

This section of the book is a note from the publisher to share the Gospel of Jesus Christ and invite you, the reader, into a relationship with Him. The reason for this invitation is simple: We want every human being alive to go to Heaven. If you made a decision to receive Christ as Savior today, please reach out to us at CalledWriters.com and let us know.

We want to celebrate with you, and also help you with next steps. God bless you!

Recent Releases from Called Writers

Recent Releases from Called Writers

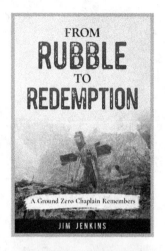

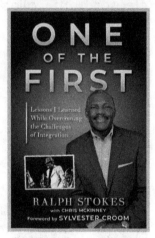

Recent Releases from Called Writers

Recent Releases from Called Writers

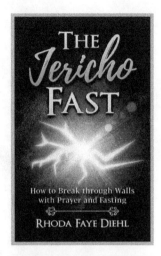

About the Author

For more than 30 years, Arlene Lehmann has been helping women recover from domestic violence and abortion trauma. She has facilitated many support groups for battered women, post-abortive women, and for women who have experienced both. She has also co-facilitated for the well-known *Forgiven and Set Free* post-abortion Bible study, and has served on the leadership team for Deeper Still, a weekend retreat for women with an abortion wounded heart. She is a member of Operation Outcry and the Silent No More Awareness campaign. Arlene is a frequent public speaker on these topics, and has also been a guest on various TV shows and media outlets. Having spent most of her life in the Denver area, she now resides in Fort Wayne, Indiana.

www.ingramcontent.com/pod-product-compliance
Lightning Source LLC
LaVergne TN
LVHW090725020325
804877LV00034B/252